Covert Discrimination
and Women
in the Sciences

AAAS Selected Symposia Series

Published by Westview Press
5500 Central Avenue, Boulder, Colorado

for the

American Association for the Advancement of Science
1776 Massachusetts Ave., N.W., Washington, D.C.

Covert Discrimination and Women in the Sciences

Edited by
Judith A. Ramaley

AAAS Selected Symposium **14**

AAAS Selected Symposia Series

Published in 1978 in the United States of America by

    Westview Press, Inc.
    5500 Central Avenue
    Boulder, Colorado 80301
    Frederick A. Praeger, Publisher and Editorial Director

Library of Congress Number: 77-18443
ISBN: 0-89158-442-0

Printed and bound in the United States of America

(1)

About the Book

The process of achieving equal opportunity for professional advancement involves not only legal issues but also psychological and social ones. This book deals with the barriers that can hinder professional development, discussed in the context of women in the sciences.

Five issues are raised. First, what behavior constitutes discrimination, how is it defined operationally, and what federal and local programs have been implemented to remove discriminative practices? Second, what factors other than obvious hiring and promotional practices can hinder women in their professional development? Third, what pressures operate to deflect women from scientific careers and how can these problems be resolved so that more women will feel free to choose scientific careers? Fourth, what is the interplay between individuals and institutions in the process of promotion and tenure or other processes of professional advancement? And finally, are there differences in the ways that the performances of men and women are judged, and if so, how can this be changed?

Contents

Foreword ix

About the Editor and Authors xi

Introduction and Overview--*Judith A. Ramaley* 1

    Representation of Women in the
       Scientific Professions 2
    Themes in the Symposium 3
    References 5

1 The Individual and the Institution--
   Elske v.P. Smith 7

    Definitions 7
    Background and Purpose of Paper 8
    To Hire, or Not to Hire--and at
      What Level? 9
    Part-Time Appointments: Where Do
      They Lead? 17
    Joint Appointments--A Pioneering
      Idea? 20
    Attitudes Affecting Women's Careers
      in Science 21
    Prizes Designated for Women
      Scientists 26
    Affirmative Action--Pros and Cons 27
    Miscellanea 29
    Conclusion and Recommendations 30
    References and Notes 32

2 Setting Up an Affirmative Action
      Program-- *Leonard J. Biermann*   37

      Editorial Comments   37
      Summary of Mr. Biermann's Talk   37

3 Affirmative Action and the Continuing
      Majority: Women of All Races and
      Minority Men-- *Carol A. Bonosaro*   45

4 Psychological Barriers for Women in
      Sciences: Internal and External--
      Irene Hanson Frieze   65

      Research on Women's Achievement
         Orientation   66
      Beliefs About Science and Women
         in Science   67
         *Forming Expectations, 67; Beliefs About
         Science, 68; Attributing the Causes of
         Success and Failure, 71; Causal Attribu-
         tions and Expectations for Women, 73;
         The Perpetuation of Existing Expecta-
         tions, 75; Women's Own Expectations and
         Causal Attributions, 78; Attributing the
         Causes of One's Own Performance, 79*
      Societal Attitudes as a Covert
         Barrier to Women in Science   84
         *Training Women for Nonachievement, 84;
         Attitudes of Women, 85; Role Models,
         86; Dual Roles of Women, 87*
      Reference Notes   88
      References   88

5 Male and Female Leadership Styles:
      The Double Bind-- *J. Brad Chapman*   97

      Sex-Role Stereotypes: The Basis
         for Covert Discrimination   100
      Organization Structure and Mana-
         gerial Attitudes   104
      Job Design and Selection Processes   111
      Peer Group Support and Career
         Development   113
      References   120

Foreword

The *AAAS Selected Symposia Series* was begun in 1977 to
provide a means for more permanently recording and more
widely disseminating some of the valuable material which is
discussed at the AAAS Annual National Meetings. The volumes
in this *Series* are based on symposia held at the Meetings
which address topics of current and continuing significance,
both within and among the sciences, and in the areas in which
science and technology impact on public policy. The *Series*
format is designed to provide for rapid dissemination of information, so the papers are not typeset but are reproduced
directly from the camera copy submitted by the authors, without copy editing. The papers are reviewed and edited by
the symposia organizers who then become the editors of the
various volumes. Most papers published in this *Series* are
original contributions which have not been previously published, although in some cases additional papers from other
sources have been added by an editor to provide a more comprehensive view of a particular topic. Symposia may be reports of new research or reviews of established work, particularly work of an interdisciplinary nature, since the AAAS
Annual Meeting typically embraces the full range of the
sciences and their societal implications.

WILLIAM D. CAREY
Executive Officer
American Association for
the Advancement of Science

About the Editor and Authors

Judith A. Ramaley is associate professor of psychology and biophysics at the University of Nebraska Medical Center in Omaha. Her area of specialization is neuroendocrinology. She is currently president of both the Association for Women in Science and the Women's Caucus of the Endocrin Society.

Leonard J. Biermann is associate director of the Office of Federal Contract Compliance in Washington, DC. He has been with the OFCC since 1963.

Carol A. Bonosaro is director of the Women's Rights Program Unit of the U.S. Commission of Civil Rights. She has lectured widely on women's rights, particularly the legal and federal aspects, and is a member of the National Advisory Council on Women's Educational Programs.

J. Brad Chapman is chairman and associate professor in the Department of Management and Organizational Behavior at the University of Nebraska at Omaha, and a consultant to numerous business and governmental organizations. He is the author of a number of papers on organizational behavior, including two concerning male and female leadership.

Irene Hanson Frieze is assistant professor of psychology and a research associate at the Learning Research and Development Center at the University of Pittsburgh. Her studies have been focused on social psychology and the psychology of personality. She is the author of Women and Sex Roles: A Social-Psychological Perspective (W.W. Norton, 1978) and numerous articles on the psychology of women and causal attributions.

Elske v.P. Smith is professor of astronomy and assistant provost in the Division of Mathematical and

Physical Sciences and Engineering at the University of Maryland. She is the coauthor of Introductory Astronomy and Astrophysics *(Saunders, 1973) and of* Solar Flares *and has published numerous articles, primarily in the field of solar physics.*

Introduction and Overview

This volume arose out of a symposium held at the American Association for the Advancement of Science (AAAS) annual meeting in Denver in February, 1977 and sponsored by the Association for Women in Science (AWIS) and the AAAS Office of Opportunities in Science. The symposium was made possible by a grant from the Alfred P. Sloan Foundation.

The impetus for our selection of the symposium topic "Covert Discrimination and Women in the Sciences" came from our growing awareness that, despite affirmative action programs, women are still underrepresented in the scientific community. Our purpose in organizing the symposium was to explore why women have not moved into scientific positions in government, business and academia in larger numbers; and why, once hired, they have failed to advance at rates comparable to men.

During the symposium we raised two basic issues: First, what behavior constitutes overt discrimination and what federal programs have been implemented in an effort to stop such discriminative practices within the workplace? Second, what covert factors, other than obvious discrimination in hiring and promotion, can hinder women in their professional development?

The participants in the symposium were Dr. Elske Smith, Assistant Provost, Division of Mathematics, Physical Sciences and Engineering, University of Maryland, College Park ("The Individual and the Institution"); Mr. Leonard Bierman, Associate Director, Office of Federal Contract Compliance ("What is Discrimination?"); Ms. Carol Bonosaro, Director, Women's Rights Program, U.S. Civil Rights Commission ("Legislative and Non-legislative Issue"); and Dr. Irene Frieze, Department of Psychology, University of Pittsburge ("Psychological Barriers:Internal and External").

1

In addition, Dr. Ellen Weaver, Office of Sponsored Research, San Jose State, served as a discussor.

The panel dealt only with academia and government. In order to achieve a balance, therefore, we have added a chapter to this volume on issues in business and industry by Dr. J. Brad Chapman, Department of Management and Organization Behavior, University of Nebraska at Omaha ("Male and Female Leadership Styles: The Double Bind").

Representation of Women in the Scientific Professions

Before previewing the ideas that came from the papers and discussions at the symposium, let us first examine the contention that women are not represented as fully as they should be in the scientific professions.

1. Women have not benefited to the same extent as men from the educational bloom that has occurred since World War II. Even though women tend to have higher grades and test scores than men, they still represent only 1 out of 8 entrants to graduate schools (1). What is more, statistical projections into the 1980's predict that the tendency for women to be underrepresented in graduate training programs will continue (2).

2. It is commonly assumed that women now have an advantage over their male colleagues both in acquiring jobs and in preferred advancement when hired. The statistics do not support this assumption. Although the years between 1968 and 1973 were a period of active application of affirmative action programs, by 1973, women constituted only 20% of the total roster of faculty members and administrators in the colleges and universities in this country—a bare increase of 1% over their representation in 1968 (3).

Of the women faculty hired by colleges and universities, only one-third are tenured, while two-thirds of the men are tenured (4). Part of this imbalance in professional advancement is due to the fact that women are more likely to occupy non-tenure track positions or part time appointments. Part of the problem may also lie in the delay between hiring and eligibility for tenure. Colleges and universities came under affirmative action guidelines in 1972 with the passage of Title IX of the Education Amendment Act. Since the average length of time between appointment to a position and tenure is seven years, women hired under affirmative action programs will come up for tenure beginning in 1979 or 1980. In a period of academic retrenchment, their chances of getting tenure are dwindling.

3. The available pool of qualified women candidates
for both junior and senior scientific positions is not expanding. According to a 1975 report of the Scientific Manpower Commission (5), of the almost 210,000 science and
engineering Ph.D.'s in the United States, 92.1% are male.
The proportion of women enrolled and graduating in these
fields has not even returned to the levels of the 1920's
when women earned 16% of all doctorates compared with 13% in
1974.

4. Women are not given preference in hiring. In 1973,
women earned 10.6% of the doctorates in mathematics but by
January 1974, in a sample of 20 leading universities, only
6.7% of the full time mathematicians were women. The overall unemployment rate in the sciences for women is four
times higher than for men with comparable training. According
to the Scientific Manpower Commission Report (5), the
position of new women PhD's in a falling employment market
has deteriorated over the past five years although both industry and academia have been subject to affirmative action
guidelines.

Themes in the Symposium

Why have women failed to enter the professions, despite
public legislation aimed at achieving equal opportunity?
The realization is slowly emerging that discrimination
exists in the very form of society, in the organizational
structure of business, government and academia, and in the
internal expectations of women themselves. The discrimination we are speaking of is often subtle, rarely conscious,
and therefore, difficult to confront and change. It is this
hidden set of assumptions about how men and women should behave and the goals that they set themselves that constitutes
"covert discrimination"; covert discrimination alters the
atmosphere in which people work and interact. Day after day,
in small and often immeasurable ways, such attitudes can
affect the likelihood that a given man or woman will succeed
professionally. It is this process that is examined
throughout this volume.

Three key themes emerge from the papers you will read:
First, most women who choose a scientific profession run the
risk of defining themselves, or finding themselves defined,
as socially deviant. By this we mean that women who try to
balance a professional and private life, who choose to
assume positions of authority, who seek to exercise decision-
making ability, are running against the usual stereotypic
views of women as nurturing wives and mothers whose main
strengths lie in emotional rapport and in the maintenance of

a loving environment for others. This tension can cause
problems.

A second theme is the relationship between our assumptions about male and female behavior and the ways in which
performance is evaluated. For example, how do we judge
competence? Is there more than one way to approach problem-
solving; and do men and women differ in their approach to
managerial tasks? Are both styles, if they can be distinguished, fruitful and valuable? J. Brad Chapman deals
with these issues. How do assumptions about performance and
the messages that feed back to a woman in a professional
setting alter the goals she sets herself and her estimate of
her own ability? Do these messages differ from those likely
to be received by a man? Irene Frieze deals with these
points.   What unconscious assumptions do we make about the
priorities that women set themselves and how does this
affect how we judge them and the seriousness of their pro-
fessionalism? Elske Smith discusses this in the context of
an academic institution.

A third theme has to do with the measuring devices and
tools available for assessing whether equal opportunity for
access to training, hiring and promotion is available. The
government's definition of "affirmative action" has evolved
considerably since the term was first introduced in the
early 1960's. Originally, affirmative action meant "to
stop discrimination". The program has been broadened in the
intervening years to include the idea of seeking ways to
help women and minority workers achieve their rightful
places within organizations on the basis of ability. Effects
are also being made to increase the pool of qualified women
and minority workers by encouraging the development of on-
the-job training programs. Leonard Bierman discusses these
changes.

Affirmative action programs must bypass seniority rights
to some extent. Since policies of hiring, firing, promotion,
seniority rights and the like are traditionally bargaining
positions between management and labor, the attempt to
achieve equal opportunity seems on the surface to be removing some of the freedom of action of the present male,
white job encumbants. The emotional turmoil generated by
affirmative action programs has led to heated arguments about
quota systems and reverse discrimination. Carol Bonosaro
discusses these problems and points out some of the hidden
assumptions and misunderstandings that have hindered the
application of affirmative action programs.

I cannot resist taking this opportunity to write a

brief commercial for AWIS. The purpose of AWIS is "to promote equal opportunities for women to enter the scientific professions and to achieve their career goals." We are, in other words, attempting to band together to achieve affirmative action. We maintain a registry of qualified women scientists, publish an employment service newsletter, provide testimony for congressional committees that are dealing with discrimination, encourage and support affirmative action legislation, take part in litigation where necessary and encourage career development by providing role models and support for women through the formation of local AWIS chapters. These local chapters are helping people by providing information on how to find jobs, how to deal with problems that arise on the job, how to join professional scientific societies, and how to learn the political and administrative aspects of the scientific profession. We want to help people find others to talk to, hopefully to end the profound sense of isolation that so many women feel. We are in other words, an "old girl's network", serving the functions that are normally performed for men by mentors and older colleagues.

In preparing this material, we sought to define covert discrimination, to explain why women have not advanced more rapidly in the scientific professions, and perhaps to provide information that may ease the pressure of the internal conflicts brought about by the mixed messages that society gives to women and minority workers. We may have provided the answer sought for by the National Science Foundation in 1974 who sought to explain why almost half of women scientists and engineers were unemployed in 1974, while only 12% of men were out of work (6). Of the women not working, only 20% had retired. The others were unemployed because of family responsibilities, ill health and "other reasons". In this symposium we have explored what may lie behind the "other reasons".

References

1. Centra, J.A. Women, Men and the Doctorate, Educational Testing Service, Princeton, NJ, 1975.

2. Projections of Educational Statistics of 1982-83, Department of Health, Education and Welfare, Washington, D.C., 1973.

3. Ford Foundation Report on Opportunities for Women.

4. Bayer, A.E.   Teaching Faculty in Academia: 1972-1973,
    American Council on Education Research Report #8,
    Washington, D.C., 1973.

5. Professional Women and Minorities - A Manpower Data
    Resource Service (Scientific Manpower Commission,
    Washington, D.C.).

6. Women and Minorities in Science and Engineering.
    National Science Foundation NSF 77-304, 1977.

The Individual and the Institution

Elske v.P. Smith

Definitions

Covert discrimination - the phrase must be defined before
we can discuss it. My definitions may well differ from
another's, so it is important at the outset to clarify my
interpretation. I use the plural definitions advisedly, for
there are several categories of "discrimination", or adverse
actions and attitudes, that pertain.

Covert discrimination may be consciously hidden discrimination, hidden from the scrutiny of offices or agencies
charged with ensuring that there is no discrimination. Since
laws abound forbidding discrimination, most remnant extant
discrimination is almost by necessity covert. Such hidden
discrimination is malicious in being surreptitious and intentional, concealed only in the sense of not being obvious to
the casual observer, perhaps not even to the victim, at least
at first.

Far more general, but often equally or even more insidious, is an unconscious discrimination often manifested by
attitudes rather than acts. Such attitudes can and do result
in adverse actions and situations. This subconscious discrimination, in fact, is usually quite unintentional.
Occasionally male colleagues or superiors with the best intentions and whose "hearts are in the right place" are guilty of
this unconscious discrimination. The attitudes and perceptions of women themselves often contribute to discrimination.
It is my hope that this paper will help to raise the consciousness of some of these persons.

Thirdly, there is widespread covert discrimination due to
marital status - the *femme couverte*. One of the definitions
of covert given in Webster's is "of a woman; married and under
cover, authority or protection of the husband"(1). One may,

in fact, question whether the effects of marital and family
status are strictly discrimination. Often they result from a
conscious choice on the part of the woman. In other cases,
however, true discrimination occurs, either in the initial
academic or other appointment (or lack of it!), or in the
later or prolonged effects.

These three aspects of covert discrimination are too
intertwined to discuss independently of one another. Given a
particular discrimination event or situation, it may not be
possible to categorize it uniquely.

Background and Purpose of Paper

There may well be those who question my qualifications
to discuss the subject of discrimination. I am a natural
scientist, not a social scientist, and for that reason I was
somewhat reluctant to accept the invitation. Nevertheless, I
did accept the invitation, and as a result my own consciousness as to what constitutes discrimination has been considerably elevated.

As credentials, I cite the fact that I am a Professor of
Astronomy, as well as Assistant Provost of the Division of
Mathematical and Physical Sciences and Engineering at a major
state university. Hence I have research, teaching and administrative experience. As Assistant Provost, my duties include those of Human Relations or Equity Officer (the name
keeps changing!), for the Division. Thus, I am deeply involved with affirmative action. Recently I chaired a committee to assess the Affirmative Action Program in a particular department.

In addition to researching the literature and drawing on
my own observations and experiences, I wrote to a substantial
number of women scientists asking them to share their experiences and perceptions concerning discrimination. The responses have been gratifyingly complete, and the letters were
nearly always interesting, occasionally poignant. Over forty
persons answered, some sent additional materials. Although
the majority of the respondents are astronomers, the fields
of mathematics, physics, biology, meteorology, chemistry and
geology were also represented. The letters I received are
largely confidential, hence it is not always possible to cite
references or document assertions. Statements are used or
cited anonymously in as far as they seemed pertinent and
symptomatic. Many of my remarks pertain to all women professionals, especially those in academia, but by and large I
have tried to narrow my considerations to women in the
natural sciences. I wish to make it quite clear that

although I have drawn from my observations and from what has been relayed to me by colleagues at my own university, the situations I cite are seldom unique to a given institution. Most respondents are at universities or agencies other than my own.

I believe I can present a balanced point of view, because I myself have only rarely been subjected to discrimination, and therefore do not appear as a strident or bitter advocate. That I could be "balanced" has been challenged on the grounds that I am so obviously part of the establishment. Indeed, I am very much a member of the establishment; for example, I have played key roles in the hiring and promotion of colleagues (mostly male!). But that experience has given me more perspective on the considerations involved in promotion. I am sometimes surprised at the naivete shown by younger colleagues, both male and female.

I am aware that upon occasion I have been guilty of the Queen Bee syndrome: "I've made it, so anyone else can too as long as she has sufficient drive, etc.". More often, however, I have wondered, "Why me? - why have I been so fortunate?". There are many women colleagues whom I believe to be more professionally competent than I, yet who have not achieved the same professional status. Realistically, it is probably correct that the same question can be raised by many "successful" men. For every successful man, there are several in dead-end jobs who just did not happen to be at the right place at the right time. It is the proportion, however, that differs, for a far higher fraction of women are "out" than "in"(2).

It has not been my intent to compile statistics; a substantial number of statistical studies already exist(3). Rather, it is my aim to discuss some of the issues involved in academic appointments and promotions, the attitudes that are encountered, and some of the effects of Affirmative Action. Inevitably, much of what I have to say is not new or original with me, but nevertheless bears repeating here.

To Hire, or Not to Hire - and at What Level?

The most obvious place to look for discrimination is in the appointment, or lack, of female faculty. Several respondents commented that they felt they had been overlooked for particular openings because they were women. Faculty hiring in the final analysis must include subjective factors, hence covert discrimination may well occur.

Before discussing present day discrimination with
respect to hiring of women faculty, let me remind you of the
situation of two or three decades ago. Take the example of
Maria Goeppert-Mayer, Nobel Prize winner in theoretical
physics in 1963. During the '50s, she was at the University
of Chicago, initially as an Associate Professor and a member
of the Institute for Nuclear Studies. "There was, no salary,
not even a nominal one, because of the University's reli-
giously observed nepotism clause that forbade the hiring of
husband and wife even in different departments"(4). Her husband, Joseph Mayer, was a Professor of Chemistry at Chicago.
The initial appointment was made in 1946. In 1959, both
Mayers were offered positions at the University of California,
both with salaries. And now suddenly, the University of
Chicago forgot its nepotism rule and offered Maria Goeppert-
Mayer a salary. It was, however, too late. Such a patent
case could not, I hope, happen today - or could it? Another
case was that of Cecila Payne-Gaposchkin who throughout the
'40s and '50s was a full-fledged member of the Harvard Obser-
vatory Council with the title of Lecturer. As such, she
participated in all matters concerning the Astronomy Department, including teaching and supervising Ph.D. theses as well
as research. She did not, however, hold the professorial
rank that her colleagues did until 1956. This was not a
matter of nepotism but a matter of sex. Harvard just did not
appoint women, whatever their credentials, to professorships.
I am pleased to report that not only were Dr. Payne-
Gaposchkin's scientific accomplishments eventually recognized
by her appointment as Full Professor at Harvard, but the
American Astronomical Society this year awarded her its
prestigious Russell Lectureship.

Returning to the present, the Department of Health,
Education and Welfare often requires that desegregation and
Affirmative Action plans compare the percentages of minority
and female faculty in a university or department with the
percentages in the "pool". The pool consists of available
persons "qualified" to be faculty members. Affirmative
Action "goals" are generally considered to have been met when
the departments' percentages agree with or exceed that of the
pool. Departments with much lower percentages are suspected
of being discriminatory. Definition of the pool, of course,
depends on the definition of qualified; one clearly cannot
equate qualified with possessing a Ph.D. degree, for faculty
qualifications are far more complex and vary with the institution. Moreover, a university department does not seek to
hire merely someone who is qualified, but is desirous of
enticing the best qualified person to fill a particular
position. The greater the stature of the university or

department, the greater the likelihood of attracting outstanding candidates(5).

The problem then extends to the definition of "best
qualified". As will become clear throughout this paper,
judging quality must include a wide spectrum of factors. At
universities, this judgment is universally based on research,
with occasionally some attention given to teaching abilities.
For example, when the field has been narrowed to five top
candidates selected on the basis of their research, the final
nod may go to the one with the best teaching credentials.
But even before that stage, how does one judge quality of
research? The importance of contributions is not easy to
assess, but is in fact a subjective matter. Young people
particularly may only have a Ph.D. thesis and one or two
published papers, and these perhaps only "in press". There
must then be heavy reliance on references - letters or tele-
phone communications. This is one place where discrimination
may occur, covert or otherwise. One obviously gives greater
weight to letters of reference from highly renowned, generally senior, scientists and from persons one knows: the
old-boy network, maligned or notorious, depending on one's
viewpoint. Discrimination may occur because many of these
senior scientists cannot conceive of a woman being a full-
fledged colleague. They may envision the brilliant young man
as eventually being a full professor at a prestigious university - but that young woman? Perish the thought! That may
appear archaic, a scene from decades ago, but in fact, it
still seems to occur. Thoughts like "women don't belong in
_____" (physics, astronomy, topology, zoology, engineer-
ing, take your choice) are still heard in the halls of
academia. A person openly holding such a view will either
not take a woman as a graduate student, or if he does, his
views will color the letters of reference he writes for her.
Happily these men are a vanishing breed as they approach
retirement.

There are unfortunately also many scientists who sub-
consciously feel that women do not belong in their particular
fields; a number of these are still reasonably young. When
they turn to writing letters of reference, they will extol
the potential contribution to the field that the male student
or postdoctoral fellow will make. But when they write concerning the woman, the letters may instead stress the
emotional stability of the candidate - something that is
almost never mentioned in the letter for a man. The fact
that the candidate is unlikely to cause a disastrous
emotional outburst is hardly a criterion for selecting her
over others when one is looking for, say, a plasma physicist.
I hasten to point out that this dichotomy in letters of

reference is by no means universal, and I have seen many very strong letters of recommendation for women scientists that address themselves simply to her scientific work and potential and her teaching abilities. Nevertheless, it is important for persons on search committees and admission committees to be alert to the possibility that "damning with faint praise", such as commenting on personality rather than scientific work, may in fact be the result of either conscious or unconscious prejudice.

One characteristic that should be included in assessing "quality" is the role the particular person may play in a department. Only a woman can be a female role model; only a black, a black role model.· That does not mean that women and black students may not be inspired by white male professors and by the discipline for itself. The concept of role model is an exceedingly difficult and ambiguous one; many white males, even successful women (the Queen Bee attitude?) do not readily understand its significance. The son of an Irish or Italian immigrant, blue-collar worker, who is now a member of the faculty of a respected university, may point out that there were no Irish or Italian faculty at the universities he attended. Nevertheless, those WASP faculty did not look all that different, and the American ideal of "anyone can be President" very much applied to him - that is why his parents immigrated, but it did not apply to her, nor to him who was black, or some other minority. Role models are important, and should be taken into consideration as part of the qualifications of potential faculty members. It is the obligation of a University to educate all its students, and by not providing diverse and appropriate role models, it short-changes its female (or minority) students.

Affirmative Action has resulted in much wider advertising of positions in the professional journals and also in journals such as the "Affirmative Action Register". Such advertising, however, does not ensure that women candidates will in fact be considered with the full weight that their abilities warrant, nor that they will be hired. We must recognize the fact that jobs are scarce in all fields that lead to a Ph.D., and that there are many highly trained, highly qualified persons of both sexes who have not been able to find positions. It is simplistic to assume that just because highly qualified women in a particular field have not been appointed as faculty at some university that they necessarily have been discriminated against. Another aspect of the search and hiring procedure for faculty lies in the rather narrow limitations and restrictions that often surround such a position. An astronomy department, for instance, usually does not simply look for an astronomer, but may feel the need for someone specializing in

nuclear astrophysics or in solar radio astronomy. This immediately narrows the field of potential candidates, sometimes
by several orders of magnitude, and thus the chances that
there be a woman within that small pool is greatly diminished.
This narrowness occurs both on the part of the search and
sometimes in the training. Students seem reluctant to change
fields, those doing the hiring give very strong preference to
those with the "appropriate" training. When, however, we look
at the work of the most renowned scientists, we find that many
have changed fields or worked on a broad spectrum of subjects.
There should be far greater recognition of the fact that
learning does not end with the attainment of a degree. I am
reminded of the story that has been told about S.
Chandrasekhar, one of the great astrophysicists of the mid-
20th century, who would undertake to teach a graduate course
in a particular subject when he wanted to work in that field.
He knew that by teaching he would learn and soon thereafter
make substantial contributions to the field. I suggest that
if one finds an able candidate, but possibly not quite in the
right field, that person should nevertheless be hired and
assigned to teach the graduate course in the particular
specialty being sought. The greater the intellectual ability,
the greater the likelihood of a diversity of interests and
capacity to bridge fields. The person being hired, of course,
must agree to this scheme and be willing to venture into new
fields of specialization(6). This device could substantially
increase the pool of potential candidates of any sex or race,
and could be of value *vis-a-vis* Affirmative Action when the
significance of role model is taken into account.

That a receptiveness to the needs to increase the fraction of women faculty does indeed produce results is illustrated by the changing situation at Harvard University(7,8).
Currently 20 percent of junior on-ladder(9) faculty are
women; these include both assistant and associate professors.
This represents a heartening improvement presumably resulting
from the report and recommendations of a faculty committee on
the status of women. In the year of that report, 1970-71,
women represented only 6 percent of the assistant professors
and were "virtually absent in the upper ranks of the regular
faculty"(8). Women were largely concentrated in the off-
ladder positions of lecturers and research associates.

It is of interest to note that the present influx of
women into the on-ladder faculty at Harvard still is largely
the result of expanding the old-boy network to include women
rather than through wide advertising. "Harvard continues to
give preference to its own people - the major difference being that now some of these people are women". Of these
junior faculty, 59 percent of the men and 41 percent of the

women had had "prior Harvard experience". Moreover, only 11 percent of women and 9 percent of men had learned of their job through advertisement(7).

Even today only 3 percent of tenured professors at Harvard are female. The discrepancy between percentages of tenured versus non-tenured faculty who are women at Harvard and other elite universities does seem to imply at least past discrimination. This point of view is well argued by Bienen, Ostriker and Ostriker(10), who point out that 16 percent of the Ph.D.'s granted in 1962-63 by Harvard, Yale, Princeton and Columbia went to women. These institutions largely hire their own or each other's graduates. If one makes allowances for the fact that only about two-thirds of women with doctorates were continuously employed full time since obtaining their degrees(11), one would extrapolate that 10 percent of the tenured faculty at these prestiguous Universities should be female, rather than the actual 2 to 4 percent(12). Even this allowance may be an overcompensation as follows from a consid- eration of the career developments and productivity of women Ph.D.'s.

It remains to be seen whether the increase in the frac- tion of women junior faculty will lead to an increase at tenure levels in the ensueing years. A problem faced by many university departments is that of being heavily tenured-in, the result of relatively easy and rapid promotions during the growth period of the 1960s. This is particularly true in the natural sciences. Many departments are reluctant to promote anyone to tenure for fear of losing their flexibility to bring in new people. Affirmative Action comes a decade too late.

The above discussion pertains to the situation general- ized to all disciplines. In the natural sciences the situa- tion is far bleaker because of the paucity of women in these disciplines(3). As a case in point, at the University of Maryland women comprise 18 percent of all full-time teaching faculty, but about 5 percent of the mathematical and physical sciences faculties.

Others(10,11,13) have already commented on the fact that the reluctance to hire women because they are apt to withdraw and be unproductive is largely groundless. The facts tend to belie these assumptions to a large degree. A substantial percentage (40 percent in 1969) of women doctorates are unmarried(13,14). As time progresses, more and more married couples have made the decision to remain childless. Even when careers are interrupted for children, such interruptions are relatively brief as the following shows. Astin(13) cites the following data: Ninety-one percent of women awarded doctorates in 1957-58 were working seven or eight years later, and of these, only 10 percent were part-time; 79 percent had not even interrupted their careers; for those that had taken time out for childbearing, the median length was only 14 months. Recent trends are toward even greater commitment to careers by women scholars.

It would seem self-evident that women who also have family responsibilities would be less productive. The data only partly bear this out. At least one study(*15*) found that there was no overall sex differential in the mean number of articles or books published by natural scientists, and that moreover, the married women were the most productive in this regard. In all other fields, however, married women wrote somewhat fewer papers than their colleagues.

What these data may really indicate is that those women who do push through to the Ph.D. degree in a science are exceptionally motivated, and continue to prove themselves throughout their careers. There may be a streak of stubbornness, perhaps an "I'll show you" attitude. Among these are women who are spurred on to yet greater activity, particularly with respect to writing papers, as the end of pregnancy approaches. They may use the time at home away from classroom and committee work to write up their results.

On the other hand, there are only so many hours in a week, and women have traditionally borne the major burden of domestic tasks, including especially care of children. Again, recent trends are for husbands to share these to a much greater extent (in itself a supportive action). Nevertheless, how can a person with major commitments to family compete with one who devotes well over 60 hours per week to the profession(*16*) when she, herself, can only afford to spend 45 or 50 hours? Though still full time, her overcommitment is not as great. The same problem will arise for men as they increasingly take on a substantial portion of the household work and child care, thus reducing time and energy available for scientific or scholarly work. How does one compensate for this "domestic discrimination" in judging quality, either in the hiring or in the promotion and salary adjustment process? "Quality" as used with respect to a university faculty member almost always includes consideration of productivity, e.g. number and length of papers and books. Many have decried this publish or perish attitude, for it has led to a proliferation of papers that should have perished. Quality of the person should more heavily take into account the actual quality of work, e.g. the significance of the papers.

Returning to the interrupted career, one can in fact argue that it is to the advantage of an institution when one of its faculty takes a leave of absence. This is particularly true today with the situation of limited funds and positions and a very tight job market. The person taking a leave of absence frees a position temporarily, which can be filled with a visitor. This visitor brings new ideas and fresh approaches to the department (hard to come by for tenured-in departments!), whether she/he comes from another college or university, or whether she/he is biding time looking for a more permanent position.

Much discrimination (covert?) occurs because those doing the hiring or the appointing take it upon themselves to consider the marital situation of the woman. There are cases when candidates for a position were not considered further because it was known that the husband already held or had accepted a position in another non-adjoining state, and after all "we don't want to be responsible for breaking up a marriage!". In at least one case I know of, the woman in question accepted a position in still a third state hundreds of miles from where her husband was located. The university that did not make the offer was the loser, for the woman made significant contributions to her field. Decisions concerning personal arrangements – where to live, whether to commute long distances or to have only weekend marriages, etc. should be left as personal decisions. Moreover, why should a candidate announce that her marriage is breaking up? Even if that is the case, it is not the concern of the search committee, though in fact many search committees have made it their concern. Certainly the issue is not considered in the case of men. These are good examples of *femme couverte* leading to discrimination. Instances of the woman's job offer determining where a couple will settle are more frequent now than in the past. Hopefully the attitude quoted in the Harvard report is also fading, namely the assumption that in these cases the "marriage would collapse and the husband be emasculated if the couple made a decision on the basis of her career opportunities"(8).

One may question whether it is discrimination or a form of friendly thoughtfulness when those in the process of making an offer to a female candidate discuss with that candidate the potential for a position for her husband in the area. I think it can be argued that such consideration is acceptance of a fact of life and may indeed be helpful to the candidate in question. This consideration is not discrimination, but it is when a man whose wife is also a professional is offered a position without a similar discussion of whether the wife can find a position in the area. To set the record straight, such discussions have occurred in several instances I know of, including my own. More husbands should let it be known to their prospective employers that they will not consider offers unless meaningful positions are available in the area for their wives. As noted further below, a husband's attitude may play a key role in the career of his wife.

It is clearly easier to find two positions in a large urban area with several academic institutions or government scientific agencies such as the Washington and the Boston areas. Isolated colleges or universities are far more restrictive. In former times, nepotism completely excluded the wife (and it always was the wife), from being appointed in the same college or, in particular, in the same department. An outstanding example is the case of Maria Goeppert-Mayer cited earlier. Such nepotism rules have largely been removed; in some cases conflict of interest rules have been initiated to ensure that the evils which nepotism had been instituted to avert can still be averted.

I believe there is a danger, however, that some wives who are professionals may think it their _right_ to be hired or promoted now that nepotism rules no longer pertain. This is an exceedingly sensitive and difficult issue. Clearly the institution or department should reserve the right to make its own selections and establish its criteria for appointment. Not only does scientific productivity enter in, but also balance in the representation of fields within the department, teaching ability, ability to attract students and Federal grants and a multiplicity of other factors that are hard to measure. Nepotism was, however, too convenient a shield behind which institutions could hide in not appointing a particular woman.

Part-Time Appointments: Where Do They Lead?

Another discriminatory aspect of appointments, which in fact is hardly covert, is that of part-time appointments (17). Numerous women have accepted or chosen part-time positions, usually because of children, though in some cases not by choice, but because that was the best the institution would or could offer the wife when they appointed the husband (due to *femme couverte*, most assuredly). There are very few colleges or universities that grant tenure for half-time or lesser appointments. A substantial number of women have been trapped into a permanently part-time situation, as documented, for instance, by a number of the respondents to my letter. They were initially appointed as part-time lecturers, research associates or even assistant professors, but not on the tenure track. As time progressed, some wished to increase their

commitment to more than 50 percent but still less than full
time, whereas others with older children wished to change
their status to full time and to be appointed as full-fledged
tenure faculty. Such changes of status are exceedingly
difficult to accomplish because of institutional barriers,
and involve some of the same issues raised in the preceding
section. In part, at least, these difficulties arise because
of financial stringencies, fewer openings, even loss of
positions by the department. The fact is, however, that many
of these women are making notable and important contributions
both to their fields of study and to their departments. In
several cases, they have become so dedicated to their work
that even though only paid half salaries, usually at a rate
not even commensurate with their contributions, they still
devote well over 50 percent of their time to science and to
the department, in fact, but not in name, full-fledged
members.

This matter of non-tenured, part-time appointments is a
two-edged sword. In considering the situation of women with
past part-time positions now desirous of expanding to a full-
time commitment, one should also take into account what this
means for the future. How will institutions react who now
find themselves pressured to give women full-time positions,
or to promote them to full academic rank, when they initially
opened their doors with half-time offers? These offers may
have been made initially to entice the husband by accommodat-
ing the wife. Will these institutions be reluctant to repeat
such offers because of the long-term moral commitments they
may entail? I hope my remarks will not be misinterpreted,
especially by those who are attempting to change their status.
I merely wish to draw attention to the complexity of the
problem, and to suggest that institutions explore the various
avenues of approach. An examination of the evidence will, I
am sure, demonstrate that the institution gains by giving
part-time appointments to professionals who happen to be
faculty wives. In the past, however, it has largely been
haphazard. In the future there should be more careful attention given to the implications, both for the individual and
for the institution. The matter of future commitment, status,
salary and tenure should be addressed at the time of the
initial appointment. It would be most unfortunate if, however, institutions could not take advantage of the fortuitous
presence of a faculty wife (or husband?) who can and is both
able and willing to contribute as a scientist and teacher.
But this contribution should not be obtained for a pittance
nor without an institutional commitment.

At present, the situation seems discriminatory, with
productive women scientists pushing hard to obtain titles

they consider appropriate to their stature, e.g. "Associate Professor in Residence", a title not carrying tenure, and having only partial university support; or "Research Associate Professor", with tenure, but salary contingent on Federal grant funds. Yet one must recognize that the institutions initially made room for such women, and now find themselves limited by lack of funds and positions. Perhaps too, the field of the part-time person's specialty is not one the department wishes to expand in. It is a real moral dilemma.

Some universities have associate professorships without tenure, or research professorships whose tenure or salary is contingent upon the availability of grant or contract funds. In these days of tenured-in departments, more institutions should consider these options, as mechanisms to grant stature appropriate to the individual.

Much has been made of the need to encourage part-time appointments(8), and rightly so. Many young women wish part-time positions, which allows them time to devote to their young children. Some, however, do not dare risk working part time for fear that they will be considered less than serious about their professions. So, to the detriment of their peace of mind, perhaps their health and the happiness of their families, they continue to work full time.

Just as nepotism rules have largely gone by the wayside, serious consideration should be given to allowing tenure appointments on a part-time basis(18). Harvard has already set the example of such tenured part-time professorships, which may, as the situation allows, convert to full time. This policy resulted from a study of the status of women on the Harvard faculty(8), and was designed to increase the number of women on the faculty by allowing this flexibility. Wider adoption of the practice would go a long way to removing the stigma of part-time appointments. Funding agencies similarly should recognize that the woman who wishes to work while her children are young, in fact demonstrates a very strong commitment to her profession, rather than considering part-time appointments as an indication of a lack of dedication.

Coupled with the concept of part-time work is that of taking unpaid leaves, such as extended maternity leaves. During such periods, of course, the tenure clock should be stopped, thus allowing an extension of the normal time limit at which the up-or-out decision is made.

When a person who has been working only part time is to be considered for tenure or promotion, it is important to make appropriate adjustments. There is a tendency by those responsible for hiring and for determining salaries and promotions to compare a person's productivity with others having the same number of years since Ph.D.   It seems obvious that someone working part time, or someone who took time off while her children were young, should not have as many publications as colleagues who had worked full time since obtaining the degree.   Judgments regarding qualifications should be based on the equivalent of full time, for this is more indicative of real productivity and potential.

Especially for those who take a break and then return to their careers, there is a question of scientific creativity as correlated with age.   Lehman(*19*) found that the peak occurred in their late twenties and early thirties.   The scant data available indicated that this applied to women as well as men. However, we can all think of counterexamples: Maria Goeppert-Mayer is a good one, her Nobel Prize-winning work was done in her forties(*4*). As Rossi(*20*) points out, this area requires further research.   There exists the real possibility that a fresh outlook is the critical factor, and that scientists are most productive immediately following a period of intensive studies of a new area regardless of age.   Again the case of Maria Goeppert-Mayer seems to support this view, as does the case of S. Chandrasekhar cited earlier.   Perhaps sabbaticals should be used to retrain for new fields(*6*).

Joint Appointments - a Pioneering Idea?

Several colleges have solved the problem of married couples in the same field by making joint appointments, where husband and wife share one full-time equivalent position. The couple decides how to share the work, such as alternating teaching assignments, or one taking off at the arrival of a baby and the other working full time, or splitting committee work and advising.   This means of course, only one salary for the couple.   I suspect the college is the gainer, for as anyone who has ever worked part time knows, part-time work in academic or science oriented situations involves considerably more than the allotted time.   Moreover, the college gains the diversity of having two persons.   Such a joint appointment, of course, works only if both members of the couple are fairly equal in stature and abilities.   One of these colleges was considering a joint appointment when it became clear that the woman candidate was stronger than the man.   The department first could not consider hiring her only.   Then it was pointed out by a female member of the staff that such agonizing would not have occurred had the man been the stronger - they would just have left the woman to fend for herself and never mind the effect on her life.   In the end, the woman was offered the position and the man offered none.   Later, as the man "proved" himself, the arrangement was changed to a true joint appointment. The joint-appointment approach is a novel one.

This type of appointment is also an excellent example of how the "Women's Movement" can be liberating for men as well as women. The man in such a shared position has the opportunity of exploring interest beyond those related to his profession to a far greater extent than his full-time colleagues. He can involve himself with his family to a degree previously unthought of. This is only one aspect of a re-examination of values and attitudes. Hopefully, such men will not suffer discrimination should they later decide they wish to take full-time appointments. Centra(11) reports that 7 percent of full-time employed men with doctorates would prefer to work part time, were the option available.

An obvious disadvantage to such joint appointments is the shared salary. Expenses for a pair of professionals are bound to be greater than when one stays home as a housewife. There are certain professional activities that cannot properly be shared, such as attending scientific meetings and colloquia. Child care expenses and travel expenses for the "second" person immediately come to mind. Nevertheless, one should not discount the opportunities such joint appointments present in these days when many highly qualified scientists are essentially unemployed or underemployed.

A different type of shared appointment is that of the couple who spend half a year at one institution and half at another. She has a tenured appointment at the first place, where he is a visitor, while he is tenured at the second university and she the visitor. Though arrangements of this type are rare, it shows a growing awareness of the existence and importance of the woman professional.

Attitudes Affecting Women's Careers in Science

Certain attitudes breed discrimination, and chief among them is that of not taking women seriously. In fact, this goes far back - it is a cultural phenomenon. Girls are not taken seriously, or rather careers for girls are not taken seriously. It is expected that girls should be good at science and math and therefore, when they have difficulties, it is brushed off - "Well, you won't need it anyway". Even today, school teachers and counselors seldom encourage, but often dissuade girls from considering careers in mathematics, science or engineering(21). The result is that the majority of women scientists - a vast majority - suffer from insecurity and a feeling of inferiority. It is widely recognized that

this largely results from a long history of denigration, both
in the life of the individual woman and culturally. Most of
those women scientists who have achieved some modicum of
success credit one or more male mentors who "believed" in them
(are they male because of the lack of women mentors, or role
models?). These may be professors, colleagues, fathers or
husbands. This, of course, raises the whole question of how
women scientists got to be what they are(22). And lest I myself be accused of covert discrimination, let me hasten to
point out that other women do often play a key role in the
development of a woman scientist - such as the rare female
role model, or the mother who insists that her daughter is
"mathematically inclined" simply because she is reasonably
good at arithmetic.

The attitude of a husband toward his wife's career is of
great importance, it may be crucial in her development(23).
On the other hand, the attitude of both to his career may
also be critical. We have already seen this in the discussion
of part-time appointments. In those cases, obviously the
husband's career was given priority. Other cases are more
subtle. Our culture is such that only recently have people
become comfortable at the throught that the woman may be
superior. One respondent wrote that she had once requested
a delay in her promotion so that her salary would not exceed
her husband's salary - was it in deference to his ego or to
her need to respect him?

I do not wish to imply that women have any exclusive
claim to feelings of insecurity; it is rather·that these
feelings are intensified by the attitude of others and result
from societal views. Men more commonly hide their insecurity
by compensating with boasting and apparent self-aggrandize-
ment. Possibly, this is an extension of the "boys don't cry"
syndrome. In both cases, one observes "there is nothing
either good or bad, but thinking makes it so"(24). If a person, continually deprecates herself, others will soon agree -
if others denigrate her, she will soon believe it. Conversely, if a person often glorifies himself, others will eventually believe him - if others extol his capabilities, he will
come to suppose them valid.

One aspect of the attitude of not taking women scientists
seriously leads to a very insidious type of discrimination,
that of senior members of a faculty (in particular, department
chairmen) not giving the support needed by the junior female
faculty while extending that support to their male colleagues.
Such support is often informal, but includes such things as
passing on valuable information concerning the research field,
help in career development, counseling concerning grant monies

for research projects, or even counseling regarding teaching. Several respondents to my letter were much aware of having been left out of this type of counseling(25).

These perceptions were also reported in the Harvard faculty survey(7). Within a particular field, men and women junior faculty are remarkably similar in their teaching, research and administrative activities. However, 74 percent of the women compared to 36 percent of the men felt that tenured colleagues showed little interest in their research, and a third of the women compared to a fifth of the men felt they had little intellectual contact with their colleagues. These data pertain to all Harvard's junior faculty, of which only 12 percent of the women are in the natural sciences. It seems likely, however, that the sciences are no different than the humanities in these respects. I suspect that in many cases the actions, or lack of actions, are unconscious and unintentional. One should recognize the possibility that some instances of a supposed lack of interest are erroneously attributed to discrimination. Senior faculty at any institution, in any department are busy with their own affairs, may even be shy, and will not seek out their younger colleagues, male or female. There must be a degree of assertiveness on the part of the younger faculty, an assertiveness more often found among men than women because of cultural and psychological biases.

Some women faculty almost feel like non-persons, for they are not included in informal departmental discussions where in fact some of the major decisions are made. They may not be included in the lunch groups. Is it possible that men still think they have to pay for a woman's lunch if they suggest that they go out together? Surely, Dutch-treat is becoming a general phenomenon, though perhaps a few men still consider it an affront to their male ego. Some women have reported an aloofness, a coldness or a gruffness on the part of senior members of the department in their dealings with younger women faculty; an atmosphere that does not pertain to men or even to secretaries - women are all right as long as they are secretaries. This negative attitude is covert, for after all, nobody is required to like everybody else. It is only when the pattern is repeated time and again with women professionals by the same individuals that it becomes apparent.

Similar discrimination consists of not assigning young female faculty to substantive committees in a department. Three factors enter into consideration for promotion: research, teaching and service. In most cases, one can only serve when asked to do so, generally by the department

chairman. Committee work is often the beginning of administrative experience; excluding women from a significant committee withholds that opportunity. Committee membership in
the national professional societies is generally considered a
token of stature in the field. These societies are now
recognizing the need to consciously include women on these
committees(3). Committee work, however, should start in the
home institution.

The opposite should be equally avoided. Many women
scientists who have attained a certain degree of recognition,
either in the institution or in the profession, find themselves called upon to serve on committees with greater
frequency than most of their male colleagues. Some like this,
even while recognizing that they may be the "token" woman on
the committee; for others, however, it may require unreason-
able inroads on their research time.

Women faculty who happen to be married are often considered to be safely ensconced in the department, not likely
to be enticed away to other institutions by better offers.
This attitude does not appear to be widely recognized, and
its significance may be less important now than in the '60s
when men faculty were highly mobile. The phenomenon goes
back to the assumption that the wife will locate only where
her husband has a job (*femme couverte*, again). As a result,
universities and colleges were not fearful of losing their
women faculty, and did not feel impelled to promote them
rapidly or raise their salaries substantially. A male professor was much more likely to come to his department chairman
waving an offer from another institution and asking what the
counteroffer was going to be. Discrimination? Perhaps.
Covert, most certainly.

Let me cite some attitudes that portray an essentially
discriminatory attitude, albeit often unconsciously:

"It disturbs me to have so and so in the meeting - I
    wish she were older and less attractive."
"We are also planning to expand into environmental
    sciences, and that is less rigorous and exact, so we
    might be able to find some women in that field."
"I even gave her a <u>real</u> problem for her thesis."
"But we don't want to lower our standards, we aim at
    excellence." (Department chairman in discussing the
    possibility of hiring female or minority faculty.)
"What does it feel like to be addressed as 'Professor'?"
    (Mother at a high school career convocation.)
"Surely you don't need a job - your husband has a good
    one."

"Well, guys - oops - <u>lady</u> and gentlemen."
"I'll give you a present when this is all over with."
    (Instead, I bought <u>him</u> the beer.)
"It is not suitable for ladies to study the calculus."
    (circa 1910)
"Women are so emotional."
"She's just another mother, but at least with some
    publications." (An unmarried woman dean referring to
    a woman scientist with over thirty papers.)

Only occasionally is the question of sex as <u>sex</u> brought
up. I found it particularly interesting that the three persons who raised that question in their letters all referred
to the same institution! Two of the women commented on never
being quite sure whether their male colleagues came to discuss
science with them primarily because of the <u>science</u>, or because
of their pretty faces, or their well-formed legs. The third
commented that that particular department could hardly be
expected to be enthusiastic about women students or colleagues
when past history included several emotional involvements
between female students and male faculty or postdocs. Which
succumbed to which? And which should act the more "responsible"? Yet to totally ignore another's or one's own
sexuality seems unnecessarily prudish.

It is surprising, in a capitalistic country like the
United States to find the attitude that a married woman should
not receive a salary commensurate with her qualifications and
contributions because her husband earns a good salary. After
all, it was that arch enemy of capitalism, Karl Marx, who
said, "From each according to his (sic) abilities, to each
according to his needs". Yet let us not lose the ability and
freedom to be considerate or generous. The person whose
spouse, of either sex, earns a good salary, might in times of
limited funds give up, say, a summer position in favor of the
colleague who is the sole supporter of a family.

A great deal of covert discrimination lies in the
attitudes held by both men and women who are not immediate
colleagues. These often lead to irritating incidents that
many women scientists have learned to shrug off. They include
the casual layman who looks at a woman astronomer or physicist
as if she were <u>from</u> outer space rather than really interested
in it; the faculty wife who resents and may feel threatened
by her husband's female colleague; the technician who cannot
imagine that a woman could know how to use a screwdriver or
soldering iron, let alone a telescope or cyclotron; the
secretary who asks whom you represent or are calling for,
etc., etc.

Particularly damaging to some male egos is having to work for a woman. It is perhaps this aspect that has contributed to keeping women from being promoted to administrative posts, especially to executive as contrasted to staff positions. Many female scientists have found that it takes technicians (virtually always men) some time to adjust to working for them. Some men never really adjust, particularly those who once aspired to higher degrees themselves.

I was sent some observations entitled, "How to tell a businessman from a businesswoman"(26), which I have adapted to "How to tell a male from a female scientist":

> The man scientist is agressive; the woman scientist is
>   pushy;
> He is careful about details; she is picky;
> He loses his temper because he's so involved in his job;
>   she's bitchy;
> He follows through; she doesn't know when to quit;
> He makes wise judgments; she reveals her prejudices;
> He isn't afraid to say what he thinks; she is
>   opinionated;
> He's discreet; she's secretive.

And then we turn to the science administrator in which

> He's a stern taskmaster; she's difficult to work for;
> He exercises authority; she's tyrannical;
> He is depressed (or hung over) so everyone tiptoes past
>   his office; she's moody, so it must be that time of
>   the month. (Maybe it is an advantage to have a
>   legitimate reason to be temperamental!)

Sometimes these may be expressions of discrimination, at other times they may represent the actual situation arising from the woman's reaction to the environment or to past discrimination.

Prizes Designated for Women Scientists

A particular example of what some have considered covert discrimination is that of the Annie J. Cannon Prize in Astronomy. This was a prize set up to honor outstanding women astronomers in memory of a woman who had made very important contributions in astronomy in the early part of the century. Annie Cannon was responsible in large part for setting up a scheme for the classification of stellar spectra and then classifying over 225,000 stars - a monumental piece of work which is still a primary reference today. The first recipient of the Annie Cannon Prize was in fact Cecila Payne-Gaposchkin, who this year is receiving the American Astronomical Society's most prestigious award, named after Henry Norris Russell. Many outstanding women astronomers have felt honored to receive the Cannon Prize. However, in 1971 it was refused by Margaret Burbidge, now President of the American Astronomical Society, on the grounds that it was discriminatory, that it was like a consolation prize, for it seemed to presuppose that women were not competitors for other marks of distinction bestowed by the American Astronomical Society, such as the Russell Lectureship. Certainly it was not in any way discriminatory when it was first set up and for the many years that it was awarded, but it was only in the modern context that it was looked upon as an example of covert discrimination. It needed the perception of a woman scientist who was secure in her own accomplishments and stature to be able to have the astronomical community recognize its discriminatory aspects. Since that time, the award has been reconstituted to offer opportunity for research in astronomy to young women astronomers.

The question may be raised, however, whether a prize designated for women scientists really constitutes even covert discrimination. Other scientific societies offer them too, such as the Garvan Medal of the American Chemical Society. Similarly there is the Federal Women's Award. One can argue that by singling out notable women scientists, one draws attention to their accomplishments. They thus serve as role models, as symbols that women do make important contributions to their science. No one has claimed that prizes for young scientists discriminate against older persons! Whether a particular prize or award is in fact discriminatory may depend on the prestige in which it is held within the organization that bestows it.

Affirmative Action - Pros and Cons

Undeniably, Affirmative Action programs and the philosophy of Affirmative Action have had some effect(27). In particular, there is a larger percentage of women in the junior faculty ranks at a substantial number of colleges and universities than there were a decade ago. It remains to be seen whether they get promoted and achieve tenure in appropriate proportions.

Another positive aspect of Affirmative Action is that many universities are examining the status of women who are already on their faculty. This includes an examination of both their rank and their salaries. Although some inequities undoubtedly still exist because of long-term discrimination, adjustments are being made. Often a particular faculty member in each department is charged with the responsibility of

ensuring that women and minorities are included among the
candidates for faculty positions, or to expressly seek out
such persons.

Some institutions have designated certain positions for
"affirmative action", only to be filled by minorities or
women. Such allocations are made informally, for strictly
speaking they are illegal and in themselves discriminate
against white males. Nevertheless, this mechanism provides
an opening wedge into departments that otherwise would remain
closed, either because they are only looking for faculty in
certain narrow areas, or because they otherwise would have no
openings at all. Why should not a department hold aside a
position for someone who can serve as a particular type of
role model in the same way it may hold a position for an
experimental plasma physicist or differential geometer, or,
indeed, a distinguished service professorship for the first
Nobel laureate it can allure? Care should be taken to insure
that such affirmative action positions are not in any way
inferior to other positions at that level in the department.
The teaching load, for example, should not be greater, the
salary should be comparable. It is also important that the
position not be used for women or minorities who qualify for
one of the other regular openings on the basis of specialty,
etc. Such channeling by essentially considering all female
and minority candidates only for the designated position,
effectively reserves all other positions for white males.

Although on the whole Affirmative Action has made people
more aware of the existence and rights of professional women,
there are unfortunately a number of negative aspects.
Sowell(14) refers to the "bureaucratic nightmare" that institutions must undergo in complying with Federal requirements.
As one who has had to prepare parts of desegregation reports
to the Department of Health, Education and Welfare, I
sympathize with this description, but as yet I see no clear
alternative. Good will, good words and good intentions have
not sufficed in the past. Working on these reports and
complying with the guidelines does raise one's consciousness
and makes one more alert to the needs. It is not clear,
however, that those who do not have good intentions cannot
continue as they have in the past, circumventing the regulations by means of the "charades" that Sowell refers to.

One such charade is to advertise positions for which one
has already selected the successful candidate, or to invite
persons for interviews one has no intention of hiring. I
have already referred to the fact that the "pool" of qualified
persons in a particular narrow specialty may be very small.
To discuss Affirmative Action goals for these is ludicrous.

What about the effect on the individual? When a woman or minority person is hired, the unsuccessful candidates tend to cry "reverse discrimination". In such cases, the new colleagues tend to think that the person was not really among the best qualified, but was hired because of Affirmative Action. Hardly an auspicious beginning for a good working relationship! In some cases those assumptions are correct. The person was hired because she was the most qualified woman available, not necessarily the most qualified (however that is defined!) person. That knowledge or suspicion can hardly assuage her feelings of insecurity. Whatever the truth of the particular case, such an attitude is discriminatory. The situation aggravates the already difficult role of the "token" woman or role model, and puts an enormous burden on her(28). She has to prove herself to her colleagues and to her students, not only for herself, but also for the sake of other women. If she "fails" in any way, or does not live up to expectations, those who had reservations will say "I told you so", and others will tend to think that women are not after all the equal of their male colleagues. There is danger of a backlash, including a negative effect on students who see a less than ideal role model. In actual fact, I do not believe that the negative effect of a mediocre woman is really all that serious, but the fear of being mediocre and the assumption by others that she is could be devasting to the individual.

What really constitutes a role model? Are not all faculty role models of some kind? Many of us are uncomfortable with the thought of being role models, partly because of the weight of responsibility the term connotes, and partly because we just want to be ourselves and "do our own thing". The University of Maryland Astronomy Program has had a disproportionately larger number of women graduate students - disproportionate in comparison with astronomy departments elsewhere. I have sometimes been asked whether this is not because I serve as a role model. This, I emphatically deny. I attribute the phenomenon to the fact that the directors and most other male colleagues have looked upon all students and professionals primarily as human beings, as students and as colleagues, and not necessarily as either women or men. It is these persons who should serve as role models to their colleagues!

Miscellanea

I have restricted myself largely to academia, but before closing I wish to note that the few responses from present or past Federal government employees present a mixed picture. Some moved from academia to government, and found the latter

less discriminatory. Others found themselves considered more
expendable than their male colleagues by the agency when the
time came to reduce staff. As in universities, few women have
risen to high administrative posts in Federal agencies. In
both types of institutions, of course, one can argue that
excellence in research does not necessarily mean excellence in
administration. Further data are needed to document discrimination.

I have already indicated that my own consciousness has
been raised by preparing this paper. Some have suggested I
have become radicalized. Certainly my eyes have been opened.
I now recognize incidents in my own career that in retrospect
were in a sense discriminatory.

Since the subject of the paper was discrimination, I
have sought out those instances that appeared to be indicative
of discrimination. I wish to emphasize, however, that a
substantial number of women scientists, and I include myself
in that group, do not feel they have been seriously discriminated against. Several in fact attribute part of the present
"success" to their being women; some, but by no means all,
feel this is a result of Affirmative Action.

Hopefully, more and more young women will have the
attitude reputedly expressed by one of the first women
selected to be a Rhodes scholar, namely that she "has never
had to come to terms as a minority because she had not been
discriminated against"(29). Complacency? Perhaps. But it
is the type of complacency found among the "Queen Bees", and
as long as the members increase, I have no problem with this
attitude. However, when that young woman attains a position
where she directly influences others, I hope that she will
recognize her own special role. Those who fought on her
behalf to open the previously male bastions, of course, de-
serve credit, and like to be recognized (don't we all?). In
the meantime, her attitude represents a certain healthy
elitism and an absence of some of that insecurity which has
been a deterrent to other women.

Conclusion and Recommendations

Much of the foregoing applies to women as a whole, and
not just to women in the sciences. The situation in the
sciences is greatly aggravated, however, because there are
proportionally so few women scientists. I have only
incidentally addressed the question of why there are so few,
for others(3,23) have discussed this matter already. Yet my
first recommendation pertains to this phenomenon. Other
suggestions concern the hiring of women scientists in a

non-discriminatory manner and with the goal of increasing
their numbers among university and college faculties. The
last remarks deal with attitudes and related matters. These
are my recommendations:

1. Society must come to recognize that many women are or wish
to be serious scientists. Thus, they should be taken seriously both as students and as colleagues. Moreover, we as
scientists must make sure that teachers, counselors and
parents encourage girls in any expressed interest and ability
in mathematics and science. This statement may be trite, but
still needs repeating.

2. The role model aspect (using the phrase loosely) must be
taken into account in hiring faculty, even to the extent of
designating affirmative action positions. The presence of
women scientists on the faculty will demonstrate to the female
students that their aspirations are realistic. The presence
of women will also help to eradicate some of the discriminatory attitudes of male colleagues. Finally, women may possibly bring new and different perspectives and approaches to
scientific research and teaching.

3. Possible avenues that will increase the proportion of
women faculty in a non-discriminatory manner include the
following provisions for married women with children to
counteract the effects of *femme couverte*.

(a) Allow generous leaves of absence for on-ladder faculty
for maternity reasons. Suitable extensions of time limits
should be made concerning tenure decisions. Note that with a
faculty member on leave, the department increases its flexibility in bringing in visitors.

(b) Part-time appointments should be permitted on the
tenure, on-ladder track <u>without stigma</u>. Again, extensions of
the time limits for tenure decision may be appropriate.
Similar provisions should be made with civil service appointments. Such part-time appointments recognize the strong
commitment and dedication of women to their science without
forcing the pace. Child care can be a part-time job, but
then the second job should also be part time. Government
funding agencies should also recognize this and enunciate a
policy that they will support part-time principal
investigators.

(c) Clearly not all appointments can be on the tenure
track, but appointments as research associates or lecturers
should at the outset discuss the future status and

possibilities. Here, too, ample part-time opportunities
should exist, including Federal grants.

4. When considering candidates for faculty appointments,
overall ability and the role that the person would play in
the department should be weighed in conjunction with the
particular specialty. If the specialty is not that being
sought, explore whether the person is amenable to the idea of
changing fields of interest (within reasonable limits).

   (a) Research should be done on whether the greatest
scientific productivity is a function of a person's age or of
newness to the field.

5. If a particular person appears to be someone the department is interested in hiring, do not let marital status or
distance be a deterrent (but do not make meaningless offers
either).

6. In the final phases of hiring faculty of _either_ sex,
chances of persuading a particular candidate to accept an
offer will improve if possibilities for the spouse are also
explored. Because of past history of _femme couverte_, when
addressing women, be sure to let them know this is done for
all candidates.

7. Joint or shared appointments may be considered as a viable
option in these days of a limited job market. I urge flexibility in such appointments.

8. Women scientists, whether faculty or not, should be
assigned to meaningful committee work. This broadens the
perspective of the committee and experiences of the woman, as
well as helping her serve as a type of role model.

9. Senior faculty should take time to seek out their junior
colleagues, but especially the women among them, who _may_ be
somewhat shier than her male peers.

10. Women scientists should themselves participate without
waiting to be asked, not stridently or agressively, but just
by letting people know they are there. Above all, keep or
develop a sense of perspective and a sense of humor.

References and Notes

1. I am grateful to Catherine D. Garmany for drawing my
    attention to this particular definition of covert.
2. H. S. Astin in _Academic Women on the Move_, A. S. Rossi
    and A. Calderwood, Eds. (Russell Sage Foundation, New

York, 1973), p. 139; A. E. Bayer and H. S. Astin, Science 188, 796 (1975); M. Kilson, Signs: Journal of Women in Culture and Society 1, 935 (1976); T. Connolly, E. L. Burks and J. L. Rogers, The Woman Professional in Science and Engineering: An Empirical Study of Key Career Decisions, Report to the N.S.F., Georgia Institute of Technology (1976); See also references in note 3.

3.   For example, "Women in Physics", report of the Committee on Women in Physics of the American Physical Society, Bull. Am. Phys. Soc. II 17, 740 (1972); "Women in Astronomy" Report to the Council of the AAS from the Working Group on the Status of Women in Astronomy, Bull. Am. Astr. Soc. 6, 412 (1974); R. G. Montanelli and S. A. Mamrak, Comm. of Assoc. for Computing Machinery 19, 578 (1976); E. R. Kashket, M. L. Robbins, L. Leive and A. S. Huang, Science 183, 488 (1974); J. L. McCarthy and D. Wolfle, Science 189, 856 (1975).

4.   J. Dash, A Life of One's Own (Harper & Row, Publ., New York, 1973).

5.   R. A. Lester, Antibias Regulation of Universities: Faculty Problems and Their Solutions (McGraw Hill Book Co., 1974). Lester discusses at length the problems related to availability and utilization analyses and the matter of qualifications. One should be cautioned, however, against accepting his arguments in their entirety as suggesting that there has been little or no discrimination in academia. As documented by other references cited here and in this paper itself, there is ample evidence that discrimination has occurred. For a thoughtful critique of Lester's book, see L. Bienen, A. Ostriker and J. P. Ostriker, "Sex Discrimination in the Universities: Faculty Problems and No Solution", Women's Rights Law Reporter 2, 3 (1975).

6.   G. Wallerstein makes some suggestions that are a variation of this theme and for a different purpose. See "Faculty Changing Departments: Why, Who, and When?" Am. Assoc. Univ. Professors Bull. 62, (1976).

7.   U. W. Goodenough and C. S. Wisdom, Radcliffe Quarterly 62, 5 (1976).

8.   Report of the Committee on the Status of Women in the Faculty of Arts and Sciences, Harvard University (1971). See also "Goals for Affirmative Action", D. R. Herschbach, F. A. Houle and F. A. Sullivan, Chemical and Engineering News 54, 3 (1976). I am indebted to Dr. D. R. Herschbach for sending me a copy of this report and for providing me with related information.

9.   On-ladder is defined as referring to the professorial ranks leading to tenure as contrasted with off-ladder appointments such as research associates and lecturers.

10. L. Bienen, A. Ostriker and J. P. Ostriker, <u>Women's Rights Law Reporter</u> <u>2</u>, 3 (1975).

11. J. A. Centra, <u>Women, Men and the Doctorate</u>, Educational Testing Service, Princeton, New Jersey (1974).

12. To be completely valid, this extrapolation should really be based on a comparison of percentages of men and women who received Ph.D.'s in that era who now are tenured professors at the institutions in question. Such data were not available to me.

13. H. S. Astin in <u>Academic Women on the Move</u>, A. S. Rossi and A. Calderwood, Eds. (Russell Sage Foundation, New York, 1973), chap. 7.

14. T. Sowell, <u>The Public Interest</u>, Winter (1976).

15. R. J. Simon, S. M. Clark and K. Galway, <u>Social Problems</u> <u>15</u>, 221 (1967).

16. A number of surveys of time devoted to the job by university professors, such as that conducted at the University of Maryland, have shown that the majority spend over 60 hours per week.

17. I restrict myself here to part-time opportunities of persons who do not hold other paid positions. Specifically excluded, therefore, are the large number of persons who augment their incomes by taking part-time teaching or other jobs. At the University of Maryland, for example, many government or industry employees teach on a part-time basis at the continuing education or evening branch of the University (University College). Others teach a course in their speciality on the main College Park campus.

18. The Carnegie Commission on Higher Education <u>Opportunities for Women in Higher Education</u> (McGraw-Hill Book Co., 1973) makes a similar recommendation.

19. H. C. Lehman, <u>Age and Achievement</u> as quoted by A. S. Rossi, <u>Women and the Scientific Professors</u>, J. A. Mattfeld and C. G. Van Aken, Eds. (The M.I.T. Press, Cambridge, 1964).

20. A. S. Rossi, <u>op</u> <u>cit</u> in 19 and <u>Science</u> <u>148</u>, 1196 (1965).

21. See, for example, J. Ernest, <u>Mathematics and Sex</u>, Am. Math Monthly (1976).

22. It is not necessarily only the presence of women faculty serving as role models that influences women students to continue toward their doctorates, but the fact that their intellectual development is taken seriously and encouraged. This emerges also from a study comparing the types of institutions from which women and men Ph.D. scientists and scholars obtained their B.S. or B.A. degrees by M. E. Tidball and V. Kistiakowski, <u>Science</u> <u>193</u>, 464 (1976).

23. For example, Maria Goeppert-Mayer, see reference 4.

24. <u>Hamlet</u>, Act II, Scene 2.

25. See also M. S. White, Science 170, 413 (1970).

26. These were sent to me by H. Kokail, and were in turn adapted from "The Executive Woman".

27. See, for example, A. S. Bayer and H. S. Astin, Science 188, 796 (1975).

28. The same arguments, of course, in large part apply to minority persons. Since this paper addresses women in science, I shall speak only of women role models.

29. E. Goodman, "The Self-Made Woman", Wash. Post, Jan. 15, 1977

30. I wish to express my very deep appreciation to the many persons who responded to my request for information and shared with me their perceptions of covert discrimination. These responses were made in confidence; I was touched by the frankness and length with which some wrote. As a neophyte to the field, the literature was not well known to me. My thanks to V. Kistiakowsky, M. Berman, J. Sackmann and P. Crossen for leading me to some key references. A number of colleagues, primarily at the University of Maryland, read and commented upon an earlier draft to the paper. I am grateful to all of them for taking the time to do so, and have incorporated their suggestions as appropriate. Special mentions go to M. Berman and G. Westerhout.

2

Setting Up an
Affirmative Action Program

Leonard J. Biermann

Editorial Comments

The office of Federal Contract Compliance (OFCC) is
housed in the U.S. Department of Labor under Employment
Standards Administration and is charged with enforcing Executive Orders 11236 and 11375. These Orders prohibit Federal
Contractors from employment discrimination on the basis of
color, race, sex, religion and national origin and require
contractors to take affirmative action to insure equal opportunity in hiring and promotion. About 30 million workers are
employed by Federal contractors and the executive orders are
the only equal opportunity laws that require affirmative action. The OFCC is thus charged with wide-ranging responsibilities and the workload is extensive.

In his talk, Mr. Biermann described the original mea-
ning of affirmative action, traced the gradual changes that
have taken place in the development of guidelines for enforcing affirmative action and outlined some of the problems
that have arisen since guidelines evolved for dealing with
industry have been applied to academic and managerial situations. The summary below is based on the tape prepared from
Mr. Biermann's presentation in Denver in February, 1977.

Summary of Mr. Biermann's Talk

The term "affirmative action" was first used by the out-
going President's Committee on Government Contracts in 1960,
when the Chairman of that Committee, Vice President Nixon,
proposed to the next administration that contract compliance
would be much more viable if contractors were taking more affirmative action. In 1961, President Kennedy stated in an
Executive Order that government Contractors must include an
affirmative action program as part of their compliance requirements. In the early 1960's, Congress had not yet at-

tempted to define affirmative action and in the minds of the
staff of the President's Committee on Government Contracts,
affirmative action meant "to stop discriminating". If a government contractor took down a sign from his gate saying "No
Colored" the committee felt they had witnessed a step forward
in ending discrimination.

As the years went by, it became clear that it is impossible to provide equal opportunity today without recognizing
the generations of discrimination that have passed before.
It followed that affirmative action does mean some special
treatment for those who have inherited the difficulties of
past discrimination based on their race or national origin.
(In the early 1960's, sex discrimination was not yet included
under federal regulations).

The OFCC also knew that there were institutional kinds
of discrimination prevalent throughout the country and that
because of this, minorities were being kept from jobs that
they were qualified to hold. The government therefore began
to seek ways to alter institutional discrimination by dealing
with seniority systems, the use of invalid tests for determining employment and promotion rights of individuals, the
use of salaries inappropriate to the jobs, the use of back
pay, red circle rates for transferring and promoting employees and so forth. The most important test case at that time
was the Crown Zellerbach case (local 189); a case which will
probably serve as the model for how to reconcile current requirements for equal opportunity with the carefully bargained
for seniority rights that unions have obtained which often
have within them a built-in form of sexual and racial discrimination.

In the Crown-Zellerbach case, after much effort and ne-
gotiation a precedent was set for repairing the damage done
to workers on the basis of longterm discrimination. As a
result, in 1968 a large paper and pulp mill agreed to change
their seniority system so that minority paper mill workers
could use their total length of service, rather than seniority within a given promotion track, as a basis for transfer
and promotion into jobs from which they had previously been
unfairly excluded. Obviously this met with a great deal of
opposition since it was argued that to compensate the minority workers for past discrimination, the majority white employees must have their rights infringed. This concept,
which is now called <u>reverse discrimination</u>, is still with us
as an issue and has been the cause of heated debate (see chapter by Carol Bonosaro for more on this problem).

As a result of this case and others like it, institutional practices regarding seniority, tracks or lines of professional development (management training lines, for instance
vs. dead-ended jobs) and ways of handling transfers from one

department to another or within a department are now subject
to review and examination for discriminative practices and in
many cases minority workers and women have been given "credit" for time in service or preferred treatment in order to
achieve compliance with Federal law. This group of workers
is called an "affected class", one that had been denied its
"rightful place".

The way "rightful place" works is that the awarding of
future vacant jobs are not to be made on the basis of a seniority system that locks in prior discrimination by dictating
that the only eligible candidates for a given job must have
come up through a system to which women and minorities have
not had access. The problem here is that for senior positions, a certain amount of experience and on-the-job training
is usually necessary and women and minority workers are unlikely to have had the opportunity to acquire the necessary
skills. The Equal Opportunities Commission (EEOC) has taken
the view that the continued use of job and departmental seniority rules, or the related progression and transfer policies within business and industry that have kept women and
minorities from rising in the organization are unlawful. It
is not enough simply to put able women and minority workers
into high level jobs without adequate preparation and training (a problem dealt with in Dr. Chapman's chapter). Instead,
organizations must eventually provide an adequate support
structure to assure that affirmative action plans will work.
No guidelines for such a system have been worked out.

Since the concept of "rightful place" was developed,
there have been numerous court cases that have helped define
what should be done to repair past damages due to discrimination and to define ways of removing institutional impedi-
ments to professional advancement for women and minority
workers.

In addition to defining affirmative action as a process
of removing discriminative hiring and promotional practices,
the OFCC began in the late 1960's to define the need for applying good management practices to the problem of affirmative action. In a series of talks with members of the National Association of Manufacturers, officials of the OFCC argued that affirmative action should be approached with the
same expertise as sales, quality control, profit margins and
so forth. They asked the managers to apply their best efforts toward setting affirmative action goals and implement-
ing them. This was the beginning of a concern about defining
whether or not the numbers of workers in a given type of job
reflected accurately the number available (i.e. the pool of
potential employees). This concern led to the writing of Order Four, issued by the OFCC in 1968. This set of formal,
complex regulations defines the compliance review procedures
that should be followed in carrying out Executive Order 11246.

Editorial Comment: These Executive orders regarding affirmative action are the strongest weapons available for
achieving equal opportunity in the United States. The government spends over $50 billion each year in non-struction con-
tracts with 250,000 employers, all of whom could be barred
from business for failure to comply with affirmative action
policies. Under Revised Order Four, "the government is required to take the iniviative in investigating contractors,
determining whether they are in compliance, and if compliance
is not achieved within a specified time period, invoking economic sanctions". (The Spokeswoman, Vol. 7, No.4:1, October
15, 1976). This initiative makes Revised Order 4 very different from the compliance review system developed under
Title VII of the Civil Rights Act which is enforced by the
Equal Employment Opportunity Commission (EEOC). EEOC can
only act after a complaint is filed.

Having been involved in the writing of executive # 4 order, Mr. Biermann remarked that when it was issued it generated a tremendously adverse response on Capitol Hill. Many
senators took great objection to it because they felt it set
up a quota system, telling contractors that they had to employ a certain number of people in each minority group, regardless of qualifications. Confusion over the concept of a
quota system and all that it implies still exists (see chapter by Carol Bonosaro).

In response to these reactions, Order Four was removed
and a revised Order 4 issued in May 1968. In the revised order, eight criteria were listed to be used in measuring the
number of qualified and available people to be employed in a
particular job or job class. These measures included the
numbers graduating from trade schools, from industry training
programs, the turnover within a given job, the numbers possessing necessary skills, the number available and trainable
in the population and in the work force locally and so on.
If the number of minority workers employed in a particular
job did not match the percentage of that group available for
the job, the contractors were said to be under-utilizing that
group. The idea was developing that affirmative action did
not just mean "to stop discrimination"; it also meant to seek
actively to overcome the problems of past discrimination and
under-utilization. The employer was now being asked to determine whether under-utilization was occurring and, if so,
to develop a time table to reach full utilization as soon as
possible.

This is the position the OFCC has reached in applying
affirmative action to industry.

It is relatively simple (as in the Crown-Zellerbach
case) to look at who is employed in a pulp and paper mill and
to see that minority employees are concentrated in the wood
room and the wood yard and are not working in the pulp or

paper mill rooms or the powerhouse. It is simple enough then
to say to the contractor "Everybody has the same qualifications upon entering, namely hardly any qualifications at all.
Take down your seniority barriers, offer special training
programs and allow those employees to move into jobs they
would be occupying if it were not for discrimination". The
issue of redress of old patterns of discrimination in those
kinds of industrial settings involves collective bargaining
but does not involve to any great extent job qualifications.

Although it is difficult to define the available pool
of industrial workers under affirmative action, it is not impossible, for instance, the available workers for a steel
mill in Gary, Indiana, resembles very much the composition of
the local population, a statistic available from census figures. In an industrial setting it is therefore not too hard
to define whether a particular minority is being under-uti-
lized. What has happened since the infant years of the affirmative action program ans since the development of the affirmative action program aimed primarily at industry is that
the cutting edge today has changed from blue collar jobs to
managerial and academic positions. A second problem is that
the emphasis has shifted from racial discrimination to sexual
discrimination as a focus for affirmative action. As a result, many of the tools developed for enforcing affirmative
action in blue collar industries simply do not work very well
when applied outside of industry. This all became painfully
clear in 1975 when HEW was applying compliance regulations to
the University of California at Berkeley. According to OFCC
guidelines, the university was supposed to define job groups
(clusters of similar jobs in terms of content, wage rates,
potentials for advancement, etc.), to determine the availability of women and minorities with the necessary qualifications to join those groups, and to determine whether the in-
cumbancy of a particular group matched the percentage of that
group in the available pool of prospective employees. If the
pool size and the percentages employed did not match, the
University was to set a time table for compliance. Those
criteria were difficult to apply to a university the size of
Berkeley with 75 academic departments.

The first decision that the University of California
made was that every department must have its own pool of applicants. The English Department availability of women and
minorities is likely to be quite different from that of Physics or Geometry. Therefore, every department became a job
group. HEW, for many months, bargained with the University
of California because they believed that the University was
not doing an adequate statistical study to determine availability. The final IBM printout of the compliance review was
6 inches thick. An affirmative action plan was finally adopted at Berkeley after much effort. The statistical evaluation

was properly done, the availability of applicants was properly judged and where there was under-utilization, a goal was
set. Out of all those 75 departments, there was one minority
goal set with one department pledging to hire one person within the next seven years and pledging to have one minority
person reach tenure within 18 years.

What came out of that was the decision on the part of
the Department of Labor to address the question of applying
affirmative action goals and time tables to higher education.
What Hew was doing at that time was sending out a 42-page
conciliation agreement to universities around the country
with a little note attached that said, in essence, "Dear University President, You have a contract pending that is over a
million dollars. Our regulations require that we do an on
site compliance review and assure compliance before we can
award that contract to you. Since we don't have time to get
out to your establishment, if you will sign this 42-page conciliation agreement and pledge to do certain things, we will
be able to award you the contract. Should you choose not to,
we may be able to get to your institution; but if we can't
you must understand we will not be able to clear the contract." The 42-page conciliation agreement required analyses
of the availability of women and minorities for every possible kind of employment consideration that you can think of:
salary, promotion, transfer, tenure track and non-tenure
track. Then the university had to determine whether or not
it was discriminating in any one of those areas and whether
or not there was full utilization and to set hiring goals
where appropriate and change the system wherever it proved
to be discriminatory.

After much discussion with university administrators,
the OFCC decided it was necessary to rewrite Order No. 4 to
deal with the unique problems of academic institutions and
on August 25, 1975, HEW issued their new approach to affirmative action in a directive now called "The August 25 Format." Basically, the guidelines set forth in that format
said that universities should not examine discriminative
practices on a departmental basis, but should lump groups
together into larger categories (natural sciences, medicine,
social sciences, etc.) to avoid what happended at Berkeley.
There, some departments were so small and the number of
available women and minority applicants was so low that the
affirmative action goal computed out to 0.16 or 0.25 of a
person. As a result no one was being hired at all. Secondly, the format defined the available pool as the crop of
PhDs graduated in that discipline in the past three years.
In concession to the problems of the universities, goals
were not defined for tenured ranks since it was reasoned that
it would be impossible to know the true pool sizes for avail-

able candidates at that level.

   In the process of formulating new affirmative action
policies, the OFCC held many days of hearings and what came
out of them was a reaffirmation of all the problems they already knew existed. In response to the problems of applying
affirmative action to academia, an Advisory Committee on
Higher Education Affirmative Action was formed, chaired by
Robin Fleming of the University of Michigan. Partly in response to Co-mittee suggestions, a proposal was issued in
September 1976 that would have linked affirmative action to
a program for generating an increase in the pool size of
available applicants. In other words, a government contractor in an area such as higher education should have an obligation to develop means of training more women and minorities to increase the supply of qualified applicants, as well
as to assure fair choice of job applicants from the presently available pool. The proposal has not been adopted. The
timing was bad and the administration was changing. As a
result, the OFCC has not been able to issue those regulations in final form. The OFCC is currently reviewing all of
its regulations regarding discrimination on the college cam-
puses trying to determine how to do a compliance review and
how to get out from under the massive weight of the complaint
handling process they are now involved in.

   In summary, there has been a major shift in what is
meant by affirmative action. Initially, what was meant was
simply "to stop discriminating" in hiring, promotion, layoffs, salary scales and the like. Next, the concept was added of a "rightful place" for workers who had not been able to
advance because of past discrimination. Finally we are moving toward the concept of linking training programs both on
and off the job to affirmative action plans in order to increase the available pool of qualified women and minority
applicants for technical and highly skilled jobs.

Affirmative Action and the Continuing Majority: Women of All Races and Minority Men

3

Carol A. Bonosaro

Over the past few years, we have been inundated with a growing number and variety of myths regarding the effects of affirmative action; although each has come into prominence only to be supplanted by the next, there are still many people who refuse to shed the old and adopt the new in this developing mythology. Initially, we heard that affirmative action for blacks meant instant success for black men; next, that affirmative action for women would result in filling all positions with white women and displacing blacks; and third in this fantastic view of affirmative action - that the black woman was the most highly prized commodity--ripe for affirmative action bounty hunters--and available for the "double count," (which means paying only one salary to fill two requirements.) Finally, in spite of what we know about hiring practices, the ultimate myth developed - that white men were losing out, suffering from what is called "reverse discrimination"--a phrase which ignores the tremendous affirmative action plan which has existed for many white men for centuries. Perhaps the most destructive myth, underlying the theory of reverse discrimination, is that affirmative action would inevitably result in the hiring of "unqualified" minorities and women instead of "qualified" white men.

I submit that all of these myths were and are false. This "mythology" analysis does not take account of Chicanos, Asian Americans, Puerto Ricans and Native Americans--and quite deliberately, because, unfortunately, these minority groups have been largely ignored and therefore largely invisible to date in discussions of affirmative action.

A final myth is that the appointment of an affirmative action officer represents the extent of institutional

The views expressed in this article are those of the author only and are not to be attributed to the U.S. Commission on Civil Rights.

responsibility for ensuring equal opportunity. While the
affirmative action officer is crucial to the system, as a
focal point for the development of affirmative action plans
and as a monitor for institutional commitment and
implementation, the responsibility for affirmative action
rests with all members of the academic community.

The findings of a study published by the American
Council on Education in 1973 (1) and recently confirmed by
Professors Ladd and Lipsett of the University of Connecticut,
debunks some of the myths described. These studies of
college and university faculty members indicate that the
average faculty member is now over 40 and tenured--thus revealing that there has not been a remarkable increase in the
numbers of new, and therefore untenured and probably
younger, faculty. The proportion of black faculty members
has increased from only 2.2 percent to 2.9 percent in the
past three years; an increase of only .7 percent hardly
supports contentions that blacks are "getting all the jobs."

The proportion of women faculty members, although it
had risen slightly from 19.1% to 22.5% from 1972-1975,
actually dropped almost one percent point to 21.7% in this
past year. In the science fields, according to the National
Research Council (2), the representation of women is
dramatically lower. There, women comprise only 1.7% of the
faculty. Women are clearly not "getting all the jobs"
either. These figures, in fact, appear to give the lie to
various claims that employment of women of all races and
minority men in universities has increased dramatically.
According to the studies, college and university faculties
are still predominantly what they have always been--white,
male, and over 40. Finally, since our concern is for
employment in all university job categories (not only in
faculty employment), we should note that women of all races
and minority men still predominate only in the lowest-paying
--though equally essential--clerical, administrative, and
maintenance positions. Both the situation and the need for
affirmative action are clear.

Understanding the legal basis for affirmative action
is essential because, desirable as good faith efforts and
good intentions are, the fact is that discrimination on the
basis of race, ethnicity and sex is illegal, and affirmative
action is required as a means of remedying such discrimination. The doctrine of fair employment in academe, as elsewhere, is now a matter of national policy. The Congress and
the courts have shaped the law within which institutions
must respond.

In 1965, President Johnson issued Executive Order 11246 (later amended by Executive Order 11375) which prohibits discrimination in employment on the basis of race, color, religion, national origin, and sex in institutions with Federal contracts of over $10,000. Enforced by Federal contracting agencies, the implementing regulations require written affirmative action plans, including numerical goals and timetables, of all contractors, including educational institutions.

Title VII of the Civil Rights Act of 1964, as amended by the Equal Employment Opportunity Act of 1972, prohibits discrimination in employment in Federal, State and local government, and in all private sector institutions having 15 or more employees. The Equal Employment Opportunity Commission was created to enforce this act, however, the U.S. Civil Service Commission monitors the Federal government.

The use of affirmative action remedies, then, is basic both to Title VII and to the Executive Order. Thus, if the court determines that an institution has discriminated in violation of Title VII, the court will order the employer to undertake affirmative action which will remedy the discriminatory consequences of past discrimination and prevent the recurrence of such discrimination in the future. This can also be part of a conciliation agreement if the complaint is settled without being brought to court.

A principal difference between Title VII and the Executive Order, however, is that the Executive Order imposes upon Federal contractors the duty to make a <u>self-determination</u> as to the need for affirmative action, without resort to a judicial determination. Thus, the keystone of the affirmative action plans which Federal contractors are required to adopt is the self-analysis performed by the contractor--largely to determine the extent of underutilization of minorities and women--and the resultant goal-setting.

The third crucial law prohibiting discrimination in educational institutions is Title IX of the Education Amendments of 1972, which prohibits discrimination on the basis of sex in all educational programs in elementary and secondary schools, and in higher education, with only a few minor exceptions. Finally, the Equal Pay Act of 1963, as amended by the Education Amendments of 1972, forbids discrimination in salaries on the basis of sex and covers all institutions. Affirmative action other than appropriate salary increases and the award of back pay, however, is not required.

Clearly, there is a strong legal basis for affirmative action programs. Unfortunately, these programs have not had the impact they might have had in eliminating racism and sexism from employment practices, due to what the U.S. Commission on Civil Rights (3) has found to be uncoordinated, inconsistent, and generally poor administration and enforcement of them. These responsibilities are divided among three agencies which have different sets of guidelines are reluctant to initiate court litigation and have poor follow-up procedures once agreements have been reached. For example, under Executive Order 11246, 61 businesses holding Federal contracts were asked to submit affirmative action plans. After a year, only one plan had been submitted. Likewise, problems often persist under conciliation agreements in view of poor follow-up by EEOC. Efforts, now that the legal basis for affirmative action has been established, must be concentrated on administering and enforcing these programs so they have the fullest impact possible on ridding the labor market of inequities.

Although the law requires that, where discrimination has occurred, all continuing discriminatory effects must be remedied, intentional discrimination--such as job assignment by race or sex--is only a small portion of existing discrimination. Racial and ethnic divisions in society have been institutionalized in such a way that equal opportunity is denied, often in spite of the best intentions, to minority persons. Similarly, traditional and outmoded views of the role of women produce rampant patterns of employment discrimination on the basis of sex. Thus, this kind of "systemic discrimination," based on stereotypes and prejudices, is built into the systems and institutions which control access to equal opportunity both in education and employment.

While such systemic discrimination has erected formidable and, at times, insurmountable barriers to women of all races/ethnicities and minority men seeking education and employment, it has also perpetuated institutional preference for white males--regardless of their relative qualifications vis-a-vis members of the excluded groups. Viewed in this context, the legal requirement for affirmative action is designed not to establish preferential treatment for minorities and women. Rather, the purpose of such programs is to eliminate the institutional barriers which women and minorities still encounter in seeking employment. Thus, affirmative action requires that we make an institutional commitment to redress the historic imbalance favoring white men in the job market, by eliminating the existing discriminatory barriers to equal employment opportunity.

For example, the "buddy system" of recruitment and hiring--instances in which employers rely upon word of mouth contact for recruitment--denies equal access to available opportunities to those who are not part of this informal network. If you are a white male department head in a university, for instance--and all of your professional contacts are white men, it is unlikely that the "buddy system" will be an effective method of publicizing openings in your department to women and minority men.

Such obstacles to equal opportunity must be assessed in order to formulate an affirmative action program which will provide adequate remedies for such systemic discrimination. And the courts have upheld and ordered adequate remedies for this type of past discrimination. In Boston Chapter NAACP, Inc. v. Beecher, (4) for example, the court held that an ostensibly non-discriminatory method of recruitment, by word-of-mouth through present employees, comprised illegal discrimination. In such circumstances--and this is clearly as applicable to the university as to private in- dustry--affirmative efforts to recruit women of all races/ ethnicities and minority men are necessary to counterbalance the pro-white-male bias inherent in such recruitment through a predominantly white male work force.

Specific remedies for past discrimination were required in the settlement of Carter v. Gallagher (5). To achieve more than mere token representation of minority group members, the court asserted the need for a program of hiring a reasonable ratio of minority applicants, at least for a limited period of time. The rationale of Carter v. Gallagher is that such ratio hiring will provide an assur- ance to the minority community which is necessary to over- come the deterrent effect which past discriminatory practices have had upon minority applicants. The same principle of ratios was adopted by the court in Local 53 v. Vogler, (6) requiring a union which had minorities from membership to refer for employment, in its capacity as a hiring hall, whites and blacks on an alternat- ing basis. This one-for-one formula has been applied in several other Title VII cases as well.

The courts have also recognized, in Griggs v. Duke Power Company (7) and many subsequent cases, that job standards and required qualifications must realistically and specifically be fitted to the jobs for which they apply. This decision attempts to address the common

misconception that affirmative action does violence to the
concept of preferring the "best qualified" applicant. Pro-
ponents of this view maintain that, if an applicant has
made a higher score on the employer's aptitude test, or if
she or he has more years of education, she or he should
be preferred as "better qualified" than another applicant
who--while eminently qualified for the particular job--has
a lower score or less formal education. But, often,
comparative test scores or years of education do not
accurately measure the applicant's ability to perform the
particular job. In fact, over the past several years,
there has been a growing concern that the practice of
hiring over-qualified people is a cause of employee unrest,
decreasing employee morale, and greater inefficiency being
experienced by many companies and institutions across the
country. Moreover, minorities and women have suffered decades of discrimination both in employment and in opportunities to obtain the formal education and training that
are requisites for many jobs. The court has therefore
ruled that the use of standards unrelated to the duties of
the jobs being sought, and having the effect of depriving
admittedly qualified persons from obtaining such jobs, perpetuates discrimination.

What must be determined, then, is whether qualifications are valid and relevant, whether recruitment efforts
are non-discriminatory, and whether training, job assignment, promotion, and counseling procedures deal equitably
with all applicants and employees and also provide adequate
remedies for systemic discrimination. In determining these
things, the courts have generally ruled in favor of those
being discriminated against in affirmative action-related
cases. In June, 1976, however, the Supreme Court handed
down a decision which must be considered a major setback for
equal employment. The holding of _Washington_ v. _Davis_ (8)
is that an official act or law which is neutral on its face
is not unconstitutional solely because it has a racially
disproportionate impact; in addition, there must be proof of
a discriminatory intent behind the law or official act.
This decision severely increases the burden of proof for the
plaintiff and will make it even more difficult to root out
employment discrimination. When an office or plant is run
by all white males, the fact that it came about "uninten-
tionally" does not make it any more equitable. The full
impact of this decision is not yet known, but it will surely
be counted as one instance of institutional opposition to
bringing about truly equal employment practices.

Perhaps the loudest opposition to affirmative action
has resulted from confusion about the difference between

required goals and timetables and the notion of quotas. However, the difference, both in intent and effect, is quite clear. Under a quota system, a fixed number or percentage of minorities and women would be imposed upon the employer, which then would have an absolute obligation to meet that fixed number--and no more. Quotas have been used in the past to deny employment to groups by imposing that fixed, usually very small, number as a ceiling to limit minority and female employment.

In contrast, goals and timetables are result-oriented procedures by which the employer determines goals, based on anticipated turnover, and a time schedule for correcting underutilization of women of all races and minority men. These targeted results are required to represent only what can be reasonably expected of the employer, which then makes every good-faith effort to achieve the self-imposed and self-defined goals. Under a quota system (which has recently been denied legality in a number of court cases), neither would excuses for failure to achieve quotas be acceptable, nor could such failure be justified. But, under an affirmative action plan, failure to meet goals and timetables can be excused if the employer can show that good-faith efforts have really been made. Naturally, the employer must be able to demonstrate why such efforts have failed, and this may lead to a clearer sense of what is necessary to achieve the goal.

The necessity for goals and timetables arose out of long and painful experience in which lip service was paid to the concept of equal employment opportunity by employers who then did little to correct the existing inequities. The notion of goals and timetables also arose out of the realization that procedures for assuring equal employment opportunity can accomplish little unless they are tied closely to results. Mere tokenism is inadequate. To achieve affirmative action which will redress the effects of past discrimination and ensure equal opportunity is precisely what goals and timetables are intended to do. Although the concept is a good one and has produced some positive results, employers generally have not adhered to their own goals and timetables.

Nevertheless, many people persist in defining affirmative action as "preferential treatment". Thus complaints of "reverse discrimination," in which white men claim to be suffering in the job market by the alleged "preferential" treatment being given to minorities and women, have been increasing. While an ombudsman in HEW's Office for Civil Rights was appointed several years ago to investigate such complaints with dispatch, numerous complaints of discrimination from women and minorities in institutions of higher education had been awaiting disposition by the same Office for as long as three years.

In addition, the results of the Ladd & Lipsett survey mentioned earlier make complaints of "reverse discrimination" somewhat hard to believe. These results, as well as the prompt treatment of white men's complaints of reverse discrimination, illustrate the pervasiveness of the "white male club," that system which gives preference to many white men and which operates to maintain a status quo in which all women and minority men are at the lower levels, competing for entry. Although an increasing number of women and minorities are being hired through affirmative action programs, it is consistently in the lowest levels of employment. The numbers satisfy the goals and timetables, but a closer look reveals that many affirmative action programs provide for equality in numbers only.

An additional problem has become evident in this time of economic recession. When industrial companies must lay off employees, the last hired are generally the first fired. The procedure seems just until one realizes that, if a company was guilty of discrimination, layoffs will disproportionately affect minorities and women with less accumulated seniority, thus perpetuating the effects of past discrimination. Obviously, the members of the "white male club" continue to reap the benefits of our society - the highest paying jobs, the greatest wealth, and access to the sources of power, for example - to a much greater extent than do women and minority men. We have only to look at the top levels of our society's institutions - including education, private industry, and government - to see the evidence of the white male club; among those persons in decision-making positions, those who wield power and influence, there is a heavy preponderance of white men. This is not to say that all white men are so highly privileged. They are not. In fact, membership is severely limited, and it is for this reason that this power structure is referred to as a "club." On occasion, a minority male or a woman may even be granted limited access to the benefits of the club - as token on the board of a major corporation, for example. However, the goal is not to increase minority and female representation in the "white male club," but rather to change the rules and alter the system which creates such exclusive enclaves of power and wealth. In fact, those white men who are not granted access to the "club" also have an interest in the success of affirmative action.

It is significant that the Bureau of Labor Statistics reports that white men have the highest earnings of any group in the country; black men are in second place, with white women ranking third and black women at the bottom of the heap. John Kenneth Galbraith has reported an even more revealing statistic - 96 percent of all jobs in the United States paying $15,000 or more per year are held by white men. (9) Put another way, barely 40 percent of the population has access to 96 percent of the highest paying jobs. The remaining 60 percent of the population, ineligible for admission into the "white male club," has access to only 4 percent of these high paying jobs.

The "white male club" is still operative in the university system as well, as studies point out. In addition, a report of the Carnegie Commission on Higher Education (10) contends that, although more women graduate from high schools than men, receive better grades in college, and work as diligently as male academics, they do not achieve anything near parity with men in academic rank and salary. In fact, the study reports that the percentage of women in the academic world declines at successively higher levels; and at every level, women faculty members earn less than their male counterparts. In the face of this data, how can the argument which declares that only the "best qualified" rise to the top be accepted?

Clearly, no one wishes to surrender power and influence. The opposition to affirmative action programs illustrates this - the male backlash, complaints of reverse discrimination against white men, and, even more subtly, the methods by which officials of institutions sabotage their own affirmative action plans. For example, the white male Dean who tells the white male job candidate that he cannot be hired because "I must hire a black or a woman" leaves himself open to charges of "reverse discrimination" and effectively destroys any notion that his hiring is based on qualifications in the context of affirmative action, even though the minority and/or female applicants may be the best qualified. What better way to discredit the concept of affirmative action than by appearing to focus only on race, ethnicity, and/or sex to the exclusion of qualifications? Or by hiring a woman or minority male applicant who is, in fact, unqualified for the particular job? Such sabotage is an effective tool to maintain both the status quo and the power to invalidate the principle of equal opportunity. Such tactics are abhorred by those committed to honest affirmative action.

Similarly, although confusion and apprehension accompanied

the advent of affirmative action for minorities, when sex
discrimination was also forbidden and institutions were
required to include women in their affirmative action plans,
chaos ensued. Implicit in the response of many institutions
was the view that they were unable to provide remedies for
women as they were already doing it for minorities (relying,
it seems, on the unspoken assumption that minorities are
male and women are white, and that only a limited portion of
the pie is available for division among these groups). To
solve the "problem," many institutions began to "double
count" the previously ignored minority women, aided and
abetted by unclear Federal policy, or else continued to
ignore them entirely. Rather than to provide equitable
treatment for women of all races and minority men, institutions began to choose, to divide scarce resources among
more and more out-groups and thus to ensure both the failure of attempts to achieve equitable representation and the
inevitability of conflict among these groups. Again, what
better way to sabotage affirmative action than to pit the
out-groups against each other in the struggle for too-scarce
resources - while the white male club remains in power and
holds the majority of desirable positions, doling out meager
"rewards" to a few members of each protected class? In
spite of such attempts, however, there are more and more
instances in which members of the various out-groups are
joining together to demand equal treatment for all protected
classes. They are demanding, not only a larger share of
the pie, but also a more equitable method of distributing
the slices. Thus, such techniques of sabotage may be
rendered far less effective in the future.

Commitment to combatting this situation and to render-
ing affirmative action an effective means of achieving
equal educational and employment opportunity makes it im-
perative, therefore, to gain a clear understanding of the
relationship between institutional racism and sexism and
to refuse to succumb to divide and conquer tactics.

First, to understand how racism and sexism operate
concurrently and simultaneously, the implications of the
BLS statistics should be explored. These data show that
white men earn significantly more money than any other
group; black men's earnings place them second on the list,
although their median annual income is still significantly
lower than that of white men. Finally, white women's incomes place them next to the bottom, and black women are at
the bottom of the income ladder. This rank order holds
true even when education is taken into account. (11)
Women of all races with one to three years of college, for
instance, had lower incomes in 1971 than all men who had

completed the 8th grade only. On the average, a black
woman with a college degree earned less than a black man
with an eighth grade education. Both black men and black
women, needless to say, join white women in earning far less
than do white men.

It is clear that both sexism and racism are operative
in placing the black woman in the least favored position.
Young black women now have the highest unemployment rate,
and the least access to upper income jobs. For all minority
women, such "double jeopardy" (the dual discrimination based
on both sex and race or ethnicity) is a fact of life. If
black women were not victims of both racism and sexism, in-
extricably linked, their median annual earnings would not
place them at the bottom of the economic ladder.

In an article in Ms. Magazine, Gloria Steinem described
racism and sexism as "the twin problems of caste. One is
more physically cruel and less intimate, but both perpetuate
themselves through myths - often the very same myths - of
innate inferiority. Both are more ruthless than class, for
they can never be changed or escaped. And both have an
economic motive: the creation of a cheap labor force that
is visibly marked for the job." (12)

Concern for the effects on all minority women of
"double jeopardy", of course, does not in any way obviate
understanding of and commitment to ending "single" jeopardy,
the very severe discrimination which minority men suffer on
account of their race and which white women suffer on
account of their sex. No attempt is being made here to
equate or even compare the effects of such oppressions,
insofar as such comparisons are difficult, if not impossible,
to make with accuracy. While our institutions oppress and
discriminate against different groups in different ways and
to differing degrees, such groups must, as Florynce Kennedy
has put it, "stop comparing wounds and go out after the
system that does the wounding." Thus our concern for the
elimination of racism must inevitably incorporate our concern for the elimination of sexism, and vice versa. Human
rights are indivisible. We cannot seek to end one form of
discrimination while we condone or allow another. We do
not wish to imitate the errors of our institutions; seeking
to improve the status of women, for instance, does not mean
that we seek to inflict discriminatory treatment on men,
or that it will occur, or that the concerns of minority
men will be ignored.

Affirmative action plans must actualize an understanding of the differential effects of both racism and

sexism on women and minority men. To deal adequately with
all women and minority men requires clarity in perceptions
of the different classes of protected groups. Thus, in
both analysis of employment data and establishment of affirmative action goals and timetables, all data must be
cross-classified by both race/ethnicity and sex. Thus,
separate and individualized goals and timetables should be
provided for black men, black women, Chicanos, Chicanas,
Native American women, Native American men, white women,
Puerto Rican women, Puerto Rican men, Asian American women,
and Asian American men, as appropriate and necessary.

In analyses of employment data, cross-classified by
race/ethnicity and sex, for example, we may discover that
while women appear to have reasonable representation in a
certain job category, the figures for black women reveal
that they are, in fact, underrepresented although white
women are adequately employed at that level. Similarly,
while the employment picture for Mexican-Americans may
appear to be adequate, cross-classifying data on Mexican-
Americans by sex may reveal that the women are adequately
represented while the men are not.

This kind of analysis of employment data may seem like
a large order, but it achieves several important goals:
first, it solves the problem of how to count minority women
by counting them precisely as what they are - both minority
and female, indivisibly - and by providing for specific
goals for each race/sex group. It may also make it possible
to more specifically pinpoint obstacles to equal opportunity
within the system; for example, it may reveal the obstacles
which prevent black men, but not black women, from holding
a particular job. And finally, such an analysis will enable
institutions to be more conscious of the fact that women are
of all races and ethnicities and that racial and ethnic
minorities are both male and female.

Legal requirements for affirmative action exist at
every level of university employment, in addition to those
discussed. Affirmative action plans, for example, must include goals and timetables for groups previously excluded
not only from faculties, but also from administrative staffs,
maintenance crews, and secretarial staff. And every aspect
of an individual's employment must be addressed--from
salary and promotion (including training) to health and
retirement benefits.

The need for this type of concern is highlighted by
current maternity disability and leave policies. The
recent Supreme Court decision in Gilbert v. General

Electric (13) allows employers to exclude pregnancy benefits
from disability insurance programs. This seriously dim-
inishes the gains that had been made in previous cases with
regard to sick pay, leave time, and other pregnancy-related
policies. Fortunately, there has been action in Congress to
draft legislation which would counteract the effect of this
discriminatory decision, but the legislative process is
sometimes painfully slow, and much harm can continue to be
done before the passage of any legislation. Clearly, a
commitment to effective affirmative action programs cannot
end with hiring and firing policies. In addition, the
university's commitment to affirmative action must also be
reflected in contracts which are undertaken with private
companies for construction and other services. Again, the
contractors should be expected to demonstrate the same
commitment to nondiscrimination that is demanded from the
university itself.

Finally, our understanding of the concept of affirmative
action should be expanded to address the full range of
institutional concerns and activities. We should explore
its value for creating the climate and conditions necessary
for women of all races and ethnicities to achieve to their
full potential and to be truly free to be anything they
choose - which includes, of course, scientists.

The mind-set which leads us to focus on the need for
affirmative action to effect equal employment opportunity
should also be applied to curricula and to counseling programs. The current situation of women in science high-
lights the need for some drastic changes. How can we explain that, although 40% of high school females' aptitude
tests were strong in engineering, only 1% of the engineers
in our country are female? (14) Or that only 2.2% of all
the Ph.D.'s in physics are awarded to women? (15) Certainly
these facts are not related to intelligence or any inherent
characteristics of women. "The differential performance of
men and women in science is the result, not so much of
innate differences between the sexes, but rather of the myth
that prevails throughout our culture, identifying certain
kinds of thinking as male and others as female." (16)
Careers are subjected to sex role stereotypes, and, since
birth, women have been led to believe that the "hard
sciences" are strictly in the male domain.

This type of socialization is a long process directed
by many forces, making it difficult to alter. Education,
however, plays a major role and is a good place to initiate

change. In the sexist textbooks currently used in many of
our schools, Jane is inside playing dolls and house while
Dick is out "exploring the wild." The school teacher is a
woman and the "mad scientist" making brilliant discoveries
is white and male. With few, if any, non-traditional role
models in their formative years, the chances of women and
minorities to enter or begin preparing for "non-traditional"
careers are minimal.

In addition, there are deeply entrenched sexual biases
concerning subject matter. Sheila Tobias points out in
Ms. Magazine (17) that females have developed "math anxiety,"
an "I can't do it" syndrome. She cites findings of John
Ernest (18) which indicate that, through elementary school,
girls and boys tend to think their own sex performs better
in all subjects. By high school age, both sexes assume boys
are better in math. This notion is re-enforced by parents
("your Mother never could balance a check book."), teachers
who admittedly cater to the stereotype, and girls' personal
fear of appearing too smart or too dumb in the class room.
The effects of this type of "subject sexism" are devastating.
In the class of '77 at Berkeley, 57% of entering males had
had four years of high school math. Only 8% of the females
had the same training. In addition, all but five of twenty
majors required some kind of college level calculus and
statistics background for which the majority of women did
not even qualify. This left only five areas of concentra-
tion - humanities, music, social work, elementary education, and guidance & counseling - open to 92% of the
women. (19) Mathematics is not the only subject where this
occurs but, as an example, it makes the need for radical
change obvious.

An expanded application of the concept of affirmative
action will also alter vocational counseling. When a woman
expresses an interest in a scientific field, often she is
urged strongly to look into English, fine arts or other
areas where she "would be much happier." "Many women auto-
matically dismiss thoughts of entering technical or scientific fields, believing them to be not only too difficult but
'unfeminine'." (20) Consequently, the proportion of females
in freshman math, biology, astronomy and physics classes
is staggeringly low.

The Strong Vocational Interest Blank is a test widely
used to help secondary students to choose a career. Until
1974, this test was rampant with sexism. Women and men were
asked different questions; whereas males were asked to
choose between "travel to outer space" or "exploring the
bottom of the ocean," women were asked to choose between

"being married to a rancher," or "being married to a corporation president." Males and females were also scored differently. For the same responses, a male's vocational choices were physician, psychiatrist, and psychologist; a female's were dental assistant, physical therapist, or occupational therapist. The counseling which results from such tests severely limits the number of alternatives a young woman will consider.

This is particularly disturbing considering the results of a study conducted at the Human Engineering Laboratory/Johnson O'connor Research Foundation in Boston. Jon Durkin of the Human Engineering Laboratory has analyzed, by sex, the vocational aptitudes of clients who have been tested by the laboratory since its inception in 1922. (21) Of 22 different areas of aptitude and knowledge, he found that men and women were equally talented in 14 areas, that men excelled in 2, and that women excelled in 6. There are no differences between men and women, he found, in aptitudes for analytical reasoning, memory for design and numbers, objective personality, subjective personality, and several other skill aptitude areas. In addition, Durkin found that the aptitudes which seem to underlie successful management are objective personality, abstract visualization, and high English vocabulary; he also found that more women in his sample possessed abstract visualization than men, although men and women were equal on the other two aptitudes. This led him to conclude, contrary to both belief and fact, that more women than men should hold managerial positions.

Although the results of this study need not be taken as conclusive, they should receive at least as much attention as we have previously given to the sex-stereotyped tests which have encouraged women to avoid so-called "male" occupations. Again, expansion of knowledge and understanding should be the goal - especially as this is the objective, presumably, of higher education. Elimination of racist and sexist stereotypes in curriculum and counseling are essential if we are to achieve the goals of equal opportunity in employment and education.

If a woman is somehow able to surmount all the obstacles and become involved in a "non-traditional" career, her problems have not ended but often have really just begun. The personal costs are high; she must make family sacrifices and deal with the resentment of her colleagues. For example, many men refuse to take directives from female supervisors until they are forced to do so, creating a tense environment and adverse working conditions. Some women, as well, are more responsive to male supervision. Once women

are hired, they are often excluded from informal lunches
or gatherings for "cocktails around the corner" where much
policy and many promotional decisions are made. A woman
must also maintain the tenuous balance between her desire
to be an effective employee and the sex-role which the male
judges will apply to her. An "aggressive" man is a "pushy"
woman. He's "good on details" - she's "picky." A man
"follows through" - a woman "doesn't know when to quit."
He's "firm" - she's "impossible to work for." Research in
this arena confirms what working women have always known.

Perhaps it is because so many obstacles of this type
exist once a woman has begun her career that the distribu-
tion of women in traditionally male occupations has remained
virtually unchanged, despite the increasing number of women
entering the labor market.

And this brings us to the question of research. The
study of male-female aptitudes described above is an example
of the kind of knowledge-expanding and stereotype-destroying
research that institutions could encourage. Yet another
example is a psychological study of sex prejudice and bias
which reveals the extent to which the sex of an individual
determines our judgment of the individual's work. In this
experiment, researchers at Purdue University had 130 college
students rate identical pre-recorded performances of men
and women who answered a list of 25 questions--with the same
16 questions answered correctly in each recording. Those
who heard the recorded answers of men gave higher performance ratings than those who heard identical recorded
answers from women. Students also judged the answers as
revealing skill for men and an equal balance of skill and
luck for the women. Finally, students rated the men as
superior in intelligence, but did not rate the women as
superior, even though both men and women had performed
identically on the tests.

The implications of such results are staggering: if a
male and female employee perform identical jobs identically
well, for instance, the man will probably be seen as more
skillful and more intelligent than the woman, by both
colleagues and supervisors. The potential effect on raises
and promotions is obvious.

Research which explores the nature and extent of sex
and race bias needs to be encouraged. We now have the
opportunity to look closely at the assumptions which underlie our research, as well as at the hypotheses which research seeks to substantiate, to ascertain the ways in which
racism and sexism have infiltrated even our "scientific"

activities. We must encourage research, for example, which researches research - which analyzes the assumptions and analyses of social scientists.

So, as we explore the possibilities of research within the context of a commitment to equality, we must analyze and challenge long-held assumptions; we must put our science to work to untangle prejudice from fact, exploitation from exploration, and support of the status quo from analyses of the realities of human existence and oppression.

Affirmative action can affect the entire educational establishment for the better. We are now in a position to increase and expand· the quality and richness of education and to render it accessible and responsive to the needs of all people. The potential for such enrichment of the educational experience can be fulfilled if men _and_ women of _all_ races and ethnicities are encouraged to participate equally in the education of the next generation.

The challenge which we must face is a challenge to restructure the educational system as we seek to create the best kind of institutional renewal and change. Our commitment to an expanded concept of affirmative action can produce such renewal for the benefit of the minority population, the 40 percent which consists of white men, as well as for women of all races and minority men, the more than 60 percent of this country's population which represents its continuing majority.

1.   Alan E. Bayer, "Teaching Faculty and Academe 1972-1973," American Council on Education Research Reports, vol. 8, no. 2 (1973).

2.   Evelyn Fox Keller, "Women in Science: An Analysis of a Social Problem," Harvard Magazine, vol. 77, no.2 (October 1974), p. 17.

3.   U.S. Commission on Civil Rights, The Federal Civil Rights Enforcement Effort - 1974, vol. V, To Eliminate Employment Discrimination (July 1975).

4.   Boston Chapter NAACP, Inc. v. Beecher, 371 F. Supp. 507 (D. Mass. 1974).

5.   Carter v. Gallagher, 452, F. 2d 315 (CA 8 1972) cert. denied, 406 U.S. 950 (1972).

6.   Local 53 v. Vogler, 407 F. 2d 1047.

7.   Griggs v. Duke Power Co. 401 U.S. 424 (1971).

8.   Washington v. Davis 426 U.S. 229 (1976).

9.   John Kenneth Galbraith as cited by Gloria Steinem, "If We're So Smart, Why Aren't We Rich?" Ms. Magazine, June 1973, p. 126.

10.   The Carnegie Commission on Higher Education, Opportunities for Women in Higher Education (New York: McGraw Hill Book Co., 1973).

11.   U.S. Department of Labor, Bureau of Labor Statistics, November 1974, Current Population Survey, as cited in Women Law Reporter, Nov. 15, 1974, p. 78.

12.   Steinem, "If We're So Smart," p. 38.

13.   Gilbert v. General Electric 45 U.S.L.W. 4031 (1976).

14.   New Jersey Education Association Review, January 1973.

15.   Evelyn Fox Keller, "Women in Science," p. 19.

16.   Ibid., p. 19.

17.   Sheila Tobias, "Math Anxiety: Why Is a Smart Girl Like You Counting on Your Fingers?" Ms. Magazine, September 1976, p. 56.

18.   John Ernest, <u>Mathematics and Sex</u> (Santa Barbara: University of California, 1976).

19.   <u>Ibid</u>., p. 9.

20.   <u>Women's Voice</u>, Mar. 31, 1976, p. 40.

21.   John Durkin, <u>The Potential of Women</u> (Boston: Human Engineering Lab, 1971).

4

Psychological Barriers for Women in Sciences: Internal and External

Irene Hanson Frieze

Science as an activity and scientists as individuals are held in high esteem in our society. Although some people question whether basic research should be supported financially with higher priority than human service projects, few would argue that money not needed for immediate human needs should be devoted to basic scientific research. In fact, a relatively large portion of our federal discretionary funds support scientific research efforts of many types (Campbell, 1971).

Individual scientists are viewed as hard working, bright, and dedicated to the advancement of scientific knowledge. For example, a group of seventh and eighth grade students when asked what types of people become scientists, felt that they had to be intelligent and to have a desire to help others (Frieze, Knoble, & Champagne, Note 1). Similar attitudes are seen in the popular media. Recent newspaper articles on deception in reporting the results of scientific research (e.g., New York Times, 1977) are read with shock and disbelief. Presumably, the news worthiness of these stories comes from the public's belief that scientists view their work as a sacred trust which cannot be knowingly distorted. A news story about a salesman falsifying the merits of his product would hardly create much interest except perhaps as a general moral outrage against what most assume are standard practices. The articles on the deception in science, rather than citing a common practice, take care to point out the extreme external pressures which have forced bright young scientists to disregard their scientific ethics; the message being that scientists, at least some of them, are human after all.

Thus, science is seen as a prestigious occupation. Although it has never been one of the most popular professional careers, this may be due more to the high standards ·

it has required for the young scientist and the relatively
low financial reward possibilities than to its lack of appeal.

Women have been especially lacking in the ranks of
scientistic researchers and students training for these
careers. Even though women are increasingly entering the
labor force and many women now plan to work all or most of
their adult lives outside the home (Hoffman, 1974; Parsons,
Frieze, & Ruble, in press), women are not entering graduate
school in large numbers to prepare for professional careers.
Since World War I the percentage of doctorates earned by
women has remained relatively constant at 10 to 15% of all
Ph.D.'s (Centra, 1974). More women are working outside the
home but they are holding lower level clerical and service
jobs (Bernard, 1971; Centra, 1974; Epstein, 1971). Most
women continue to avoid achievement or excellence in careers
in politics, business, sports and other fields considered to
be "masculine" fields. This pattern of relative nonachievement for women perpetuates itself since societal attitudes
remain unchanged about appropriate roles for women and women
who do want to achieve through their careers find little
support or encouragement from others. Such attitudes form
the basis for both overt and covert barriers to women's
achievements.

Research on Women's Achievement Orientation

A number of causal explanations for the high achievement
orientation or desire for success in these "achievement" areas
for men and the nonachievement orientation of or relative
lack of concern with "success" of women have been proposed
over the last 20 years (See Chapter 12 in Frieze, Parsons,
Johnson, Ruble, & Zellman, in press-a). Most of theoretical
and empirical research supporting these explanations has
focused on internal psychological factors which inhibit women
from attempting to achieve outside the traditional female
role. Women's relative lack of "achievement" has been attributed by others to deficiencies in their achievement motivation (McClelland, Atkinson, Clark, & Lowell, 1953; Veroff,
1969), their high fear of failure (see O'Leary, 1974 for a
review of this literature) and their fear of success (e.g.,
Horner, 1972). More recently, it has been suggested that
women do experience desires to succeed but that these achievement strivings are directed toward achievement in the home or
in traditionally defined feminine tasks (Stein & Bailey,
1973). Tangri (1972) further suggested that some women may
desire to achieve vicariously through the accomplishments of
their husbands and children. We have suggested that cognitive
factors such as beliefs about one's own ability and why one
succeeds or fails are of major importance (Frieze, 1975;

Frieze, Fisher, Hanusa, McHugh, & Valle, in press-b). All of
this research attributes the causes of women's failures to
achieve to internal factors in the women themselves. Such an
emphasis ignores external factors which are of major importance in determining how people live their lives. Such a
bias has important political implications which women need to
consider since it focuses the blame for her difficulties on
the woman herself.

It is our current belief that external barriers to
achievement are as important, if not more so, than any
internal psychological barriers to achievement in women
(Frieze, et al., in press-b). However, there is evidence that
these internal barriers do exist. Since so much of the past
research focused upon such variables, this paper will analyze
what I believe is one of the major internal variables--cogni-
tions or beliefs about one's ability and why one succeeds or
fails. However, the major focus of the paper will be how
these cognitive factors affect the judgments that others make
about women's achievements and aspirations in science.

Beliefs About Science and Women in Science

Forming Expectations

People have many types of expectations for other people.
For those they know well, these expectations are based on a
series of past experiences with the person. They know
generally how that person will react in a variety of situations and they expect the person to behave similarly in the
future. Expectations for what they will or will not be able
to do are also based on a series of past performance levels.
Expectations also depend on the specific nature and requirements of the task and on one's view of why the person was or
was not successful in the past (e.g., Valle & Frieze, 1976;
Weiner, 1974).

Expectations for a stranger or a casual acquaintance are
necessarily based on other information; there is no past
history of success or failure. In such cases, expectations
are based largely on stereotypes. The unknown individual is
first identified as being a member of one or more groups
(these may include sex, age, race, social-economic class,
etc.). Since many possible labels can be applied, the more
personally salient would most likely be invoked. Then, on
the basis of one's stereotypes of that most salient group,
the individual will be expected to have the attributes and
abilities associated with that group (Ichheiser, 1970). Thus,
an unknown woman might be expected to be good at cooking but
poor at mathematical tasks by those who do not know her.

Beliefs About Science

Expectations of task performance for strangers and friends depend on one's beliefs about the task itself and the skills it necessitates. Science is popularly seen as a difficult task requiring both high ability and a strong motivation to do well and a capacity to persist in the face of failure (e.g., Frieze & Knoble, Note 2). Some examples of these attitudes are seen in the stories told by college students when asked to describe what might be happening in a picture depicting two women in a laboratory. Although these stories are used as a projective device to measure the storyteller's own motivations (McClelland et al., 1953), the frequent references to hard work across different types of stories are interesting because they suggest underlying views of science. These stories are from a study by Alper (1974):

> This lady scientist, like Madame Curie, is about to make an amazing discovery. She has been trying for months to find a cure for cancer and in spite of almost giving up because of repeated failures, she and her assistant know that this is the moment. If she drops the right amount of solution into the tube, it will neutralize and that will be the answer to her years of effort. She will do it. (p. 198)

> The instructor is showing her student how to do a step in a complicated experimental procedure. The student has been working on the experiment for some time, and is nearly at the end of her work. She is observing carefully what the other woman does, and, when she returns to her own work, will repeat the procedure with care and precision and will be able to finish her project and achieve significant results. The instructor, would like the student to become an able scientist, and is pleased with her work. (p. 198)

Other data from a study we have recently completed with college students also supports the idea that science is seen as a particularly difficult and demanding occupation (Frieze & Knoble, Note 2). When asked to state what factors they felt were particularly important for success as a physicist or a research psychologist, both men and women cited ability and effort as well as having a strong interest in science and research. Failure was seen as resulting from lack of persistence, inadequate training, or lack of ability.[1]

Thus, science is seen as requiring talent. People who are not perceived to be bright and able and willing to work hard would not be expected to do well in science. Such reservations may particularly apply to women. Many of the college students in our study expected that women would have a more difficult time being successful in science than men, especially in physics. Alper's (1974) subjects reported similar reservations:

> It is a time when women scientists are not
> common. They are in the minority and are
> often looked down upon by men. Therefore,
> they have to work extra hard to prove them-
> selves. These two female technologists are
> working on a biochemistry experiment. The
> one standing is trying to train the younger
> woman whom she feels has much potential.
> Through their hard work and dedication to
> their project they will succeed. They will
> not only make a name for themselves...
> (p. 199)

In fact, many subjects down-graded the status of the women in the laboratory in telling their stories although Alper reports that this did not occur when one of the people in the picture was a man:

> The lady with the test tube is a movie star
> who has sunk to doing TV commercials. The
> other is an admiring nobody [who] pities her
> ... They both fade into oblivion. No one
> will like them or pay attention to them...
> The star commits suicide and the other
> marries a florist and gets fat. (p. 199)

Some of the research about people's expectations about women's abilities and the implications of these expectations are discussed in the following section. An important related issue are people's beliefs about why success or failure has occurred for an individual person. These causal attributions influence expectancies and effect the reactions of others to the performance. These cognitive factors may be the basis for many forms of covert discrimination for women in science.

---

[1]We are currently replicating this study of the perceptions of the underlying reasons for success and failure in science with a sample of researchers in science. This project is being done in conjunction with Ian Mitroff and Ted Jacob.

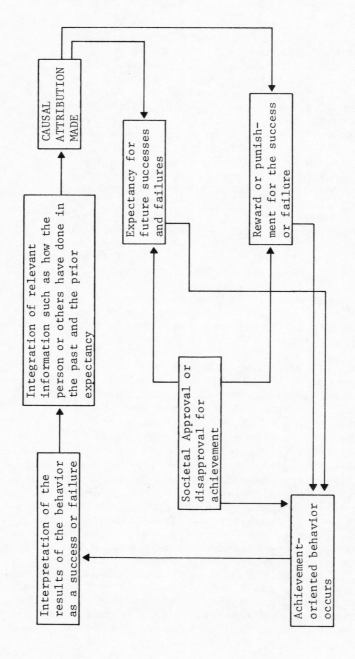

Figure 1. The attributional process for achievement events. (Modified from Frieze, Fisher, Hanusa, McHugh, & Valle, in press-b.)

Attributing the Causes of Success and Failure

Weiner and his associates (e.g., Weiner, 1974; Weiner, Frieze, Kukla, Reed, Rest, & Rosenbaum, 1971) have done extensive research demonstrating the importance of attributions or beliefs about why success or failure occurs in understanding achievement-oriented behavior. Most of this research concerns the attributions made by an individual about his or her own successes and failures and how these attributions influence affect, future expectancies and subsequent achievement strivings. It is assumed that people will be more likely to attempt tasks where they feel they have a high expectancy of doing well and that they will desire to maximize positive feelings about success and minimize negative feelings about failure. Both affect and expectancy are effected by the type of causal attribution made about why a particular event was a success or failure. Similar processes exist for attributions about other people.

A diagram of the attributional process as conceptualized by Frieze et al. (in press-b) is shown in Figure 1. In this model, the attributional process begins with an achievement behavior which is then interpreted as a success or failure. Once the outcome is established, the person utilizes available information such as his or her prior expectancy for the person's success at this task and the past history of this person's and others' successes to determine the cause of the outcome (Frieze, 1976-b; Frieze & Weiner, 1971).

There are many possible reasons why a particular success or failure might occur and, therefore, many causal attributions which can be made in any situation (Heider, 1958). Thus a person may succeed at a task because of his or her high ability, trying hard, general motivation, good luck, the fact that the task was relatively easy and/or someone helping. Failure may result from low ability, not trying sufficiently hard, lack of motivation, being sick or tired, bad luck, task difficulty, or someone interfering (Elig & Frieze, 1975; Frieze, 1976-a; Weiner et al., 1971).

These causal attributions can be classified along three dimensions: internal-external; stable-unstable; and intentional-unintentional. This classification system is shown in Table 1. Ability, effort, mood, personality and knowledge are causes originating within or internal to the individual, while task difficulty, other people's help or hurt and luck are causes within the environment or external to the individual. This dimension has been shown to be particularly important for affect. More pride or satisfaction is reported by people who attribute their successes internally

Table 1

A Three-Dimensional Model for Classifying
Causal Attributions for Success and Failure

(modified from Elig and Frieze, 1975)

INTERNAL

	Stable	Unstable
Intentional	Stable effort (Diligence or laziness)	Unstable effort (Trying or not trying hard)
Unintentional	Ability Knowledge or background Personality	Fatigue Mood

EXTERNAL

	Stable	Unstable
Intentional	Others always help or interfere	Others help or interfere with this event
Unintentional	Task difficulty or ease Personality of others	Task difficulty or ease (task changes) Luck or unique circumstances Others accidentally help or interfere

than if the attribution is made to an external cause (Weiner, Heckhausen, Meyer, & Cook, 1972; Weiner, Russell, & Lerman, in press). These same studies have shown that internally attributed failures lead to more shame or dissatisfaction after failure.

A second dimension along which the various causes may be differentiated is in their stability. Ability, personality, diligence or laziness and task difficulty are relatively stable causes, while effort, mood and luck may be highly changeable. If success at a particular type of activity was due to a person's high ability or the activity's being easy, one would anticipate continued success for that person on the same task. Similarly, if a failure was due to these stable causes, continued failure would be anticipated. Conversely, unstable causes lead to acknowledging the possibility of change. Failures attributed to bad luck or lack of effort may result in expectations for eventual success since bad luck might finally change or trying harder might lead to future success (McMahan, 1973; Weiner et al., 1972).

An attribution is considered to be intentional to the degree that the person is perceived to have control of his or her actions. Thus, ability and personality are factors within the person over which that person has little control, and events attributed to these factors would be unintentional. However, the actor is perceived to have control over the effort he or she exerts so that attributions to effort are intentional (as well as being internal). The intentionality dimension appears to be related to reward and punishment, with most reward given for performances attributed to internal, intentional causes, although further research is needed to clarify these relationships (Weiner, et al., in press).

Causal Attributions and Expectations for Women

The available research suggests that women are expected to do more poorly than men at numerous tasks. For example, Feldman-Summers and Kiesler (1974) reported that they were unable to find any occupation in which females were expected to outperform males. For all the professions they used, which included pediatrician, writer, child psychologist, surgeon, dancer, diagnostician, clinical psychologist and biographer of famous women, males were expected to be more successful than females. These lower expectations may also directly affect the performance of women. Research has indicated that when people are randomly assigned to high and low expectancy groups, the high expectancy group tends to perform better than the group to which low expectancies were assigned (Rosenthal & Jacobson, 1968; Tyler, 1958).

Causal attributions for performance also differ according to the sex of the person being evaluated. Deaux and Emswiller (1974) asked both male and female college students to evaluate another's performance at finding hidden objects in a complex design. The task was described as either masculine or feminine; males were expected to do better at the masculine task and females at the female task. When given information that the person had succeeded at the task, males' successes on the masculine task tended to be attributed more to ability while females' successes were more likely to be attributed to luck. There were no differences on the feminine task.

The causal attributions made about a person have important implications not only for the affect and expectancies of that person but also for the rewards given that person by others (Weiner et al., in press). People are constantly being evaluated by others for their achievements, whether being considered for a grade, a job, or a promotion. The kinds of attributions made by the decision makers in these situations have major consequences for those being judged. For example, if a teacher thinks that the reason that a student did well on a test is that he cheated, the reaction of the teacher will be quite different than if he felt that the student had studied hard for the exam. Also, a student will probably be more motivated to study in a class where she thinks the teacher determines grades on the basis of competence and the effort of the student rather than by chance or favoritism. Another example of this process is the reaction of an employer to a poor performance by an employee. If the employer perceives that the poor performance was due to external circumstances over which the employee had no control (such as being given a difficult assignment) or unstable factors which might be expected to change in the near future (the employee had been sick and is now better), the employer will be more likely to give that employee a second chance. If, however, the employer felt that the poor performance was the result of internal factors such as the employee being lazy or generally incompetent, the employer might well fire the person (Valle & Frieze, 1976).

A pattern of attributing the successes of men more to their abilities than the successes of women and the failures of women more to their lack of ability was reported by Feather and Simon (1975) and Etaugh and Brown (1975). Etaugh and Brown also found that female successes were more attributed to effort. Feldman-Summers and Kiesler (1974) further found that male subjects attributed more ability to a male physician than to a female physician. The males attributed the success of the female physician to either her strong motivation or to her having an easier task (i.e., external factors aided her in becoming a doctor). Female subjects in this study also attributed greater motivation to the female physician, but they were more likely to see the male physician as having an easier task.

Although there have not been a great many studies in this area, and there have been none as yet dealing specifically with science, those studies which have been done suggest that female successes in general are more likely to be attributed to unstable factors such as luck or effort while male successes are more often attributed to the stable internal factor of ability. Such patterns, if they generalize, would imply that even when women do succeed, since their successes are attributed more to unstable factors, they would not be expected by others to continue to be successful.

The Perpetuation of Existing Expectancies

Valle and Frieze (1976) present a model relating initial expectations and causal attributions which might have important implications for the evaluation of women. Her model suggests that when making a prediction about the future performance of an individual, the perceiver considers both the individual's most recent performance and the expectations which the perceiver had before that performance. Predictions about the future depend upon how much importance is given to this recent performance and how much to the initial expectations. This model suggests that the amount of importance given to a previous performance is related to the attributed cause of that performance. If the performance was attributed to stable factors (e.g., ability or task) the previous outcome would be weighted heavily. If, on the other hand, the outcome was attributed to unstable factors (e.g., luck or effort) it should be weighted less heavily. Therefore, the more an outcome is attributed to stable causes, the greater weight which will be given to that outcome in determining predictions for the future, and the closer the expectations for the future will be to the outcome, regardless of initial expectancy.

In addition, the type of attribution made is a function of the difference between the actual outcome and the initial expectancies. The greater the absolute value of this difference the greater will be the tendency to attribute the outcome to unstable factors such as luck, mood, or effort. The less this absolute difference, the greater will be the tendency to attribute the outcome to stable factors such as the ability of the actor or stable effort. For both observer attributions (Feather & Simon, 1971-a; Frieze & Weiner, 1971) and self attributions (Feather, 1969; Feather & Simon, 1971-a; 1971-b; Simon & Feather, 1973), this implication has received wide support; the greater the difference between an outcome and previous expectations (either measured directly or

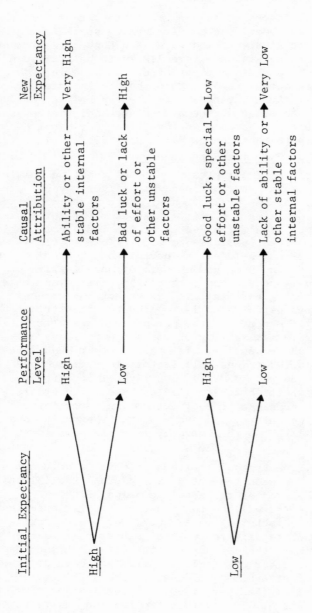

Figure 2. Attributional mediation of expectancy changes. From V. A. Valle & I. H. Frieze. The stability of causal attributions as a mediator in changing expectations for success. Journal of Personality and Social Psychology, 1976, 33, 579-587.

assumed from the information available concerning the actor's past performance), the greater the tendency to attribute the outcome to unstable factors, especially to luck. Correlational data from Valle (1974) provide further support in a direct test of these implications.

To summarize, as shown in Figure 2, Valle & Frieze's model describes a mechanism whereby changes in expectations are minimized by the types of causal attributions which are made. Unexpected outcomes are attributed to unstable causes and, therefore, have less weight in determining future predictions; expected outcomes are more attributed to stable cause and tend to support and reinforce original expectations. This model has important implications for a person who is expected to do poorly. If such a person performs well, the performance will be attributed to unstable factors, which in turn, means that the supervisor will still expect the person to do poorly in the future. This process would be especially detrimental for a minority group member or a woman who is expected to do poorly just because of membership in that group. Because of these initial low expectations on the part of many people, it would be more difficult for such people to establish their competence to their supervisor. This model for expectancy changes is particularly applicable to the situation of women working in traditionally masculine fields such as science.

The application of this model is relevant to women only if they are indeed expected to do less well than men. Research has indicated that the performances of women are usually evaluated lower than those of men. Goldberg (1968) demonstrated that female college students evaluated articles supposedly written by women lower than articles with male authors, even though the authors' names had been randomly assigned. Similar results were found in more recent studies (e.g., Deaux & Emswiller, 1974; Pheterson, Kiesler, & Goldberg, 1971; Piacente, Penner, Hawkins, & Cohen, 1974).

The Valle and Frieze model would then predict that in occupations in which women are expected to perform poorly, a successful performance by a woman will tend to be attributed more to unstable factors than would a similar performance by a man. In turn, since this successful performance has been attributed to unstable factors, it will have less impact on the evaluator's predictions for the future success of the woman than a similar successful performance would have for a man. In other words, it would be more difficult for a woman to prove her competency by a high quality performance than it would be for a man. The research which indicated that success by women tends to be attributed more to unstable factors supports this prediction (Deaux & Emswiller, 1974; Feldman-Summers & Kiesler, 1974).

Finally, the model predicts that by manipulating the type
of attribution made for a particular outcome, one can lessen
or increase the weight given to that performance in making
predictions for the future. If the employer can be made to
attribute the cause of a successful performance to stable
factors, the vicious circle of low initial and future expectations can be interrupted by changing the causal attributions.
However, the model also cautions that a woman's performance
should not be too deviant from the initially low expectations
held for her by others. If a woman who is expected to do very
poorly, actually does very well, this will be attributed to
unstable factors even more than might already be expected.
The model suggests that there is a point of maximum change for
any specific situation and that the level of performance
should be better than expected but not too much better (Valle
& Frieze, 1976).

Women's Own Expectations and Causal Attributions

Self Expectations. One's own expectations for success
and failure have been shown to affect one's behavior in
achievement situations. Several studies have demonstrated
that people with high expectations of success on achievement
tasks perform better than those with low expectations (e.g.,
Battle, 1965; Feather, 1966). While these studies do not
eliminate the possibility that these high expectations are
based on a history of prior success, other studies (Diggory,
1966; Tyler, 1958) have randomly assigned levels of expectancy. Subjects that were randomly given high expectation
levels performed better than those given low expectation
levels in these studies, thus demonstrating that expectancy
levels directly affect performance.

Differential expectations for success and failure in
males as compared to females have been well documented
(e.g., Crandall, 1969; Frieze et al., in press-b). Women do
not expect to do as well as men in novel tasks, athletic
tasks or academic tasks. Men consistently overestimate their
future performance while women tend to underestimate.

Given the cultural stereotype that males are more
intelligent, more achieving, and more competitive than
females (Broverman, Vogel, Broverman, Clarkson, & Rosenkrantz,
1972), it is not surprising that males generally report higher
expectations than females or that both males and females predict that males will be more successful. However, while this
cultural stereotype influences generalized expectancies, it
should not have the same effect on specific expectancies for
familiar tasks (McHugh, Note 3). If a subject has had previous experience with a task, the expectancy estimate is
based on past experience. However, when giving an expectancy

estimate for a novel task, the person must rely upon a more
general expectancy level (Frieze et al., in press-b). However, even with familiar tasks women may not see their performances as positively as men. Lacher and Lacher (Note 4)
reported that male college freshmen were more likely to see
their high school grades as underestimating their ability;
female freshmen felt their high school grades overestimated
their ability even though there were no differences in the
actual ability levels of men and women as measured by their
verbal SAT scores or college grades.

Consequences of Higher Male Expectations. Whether sex
differences in expectation levels are explained by generalized versus specific expectancies, cultural stereotypes,
experimental manipulations, or other factors, the effects of
the higher expectations of males still exist. Higher expectations for success lead to superior performance (Diggory,
1966), and higher evaluations of performance (Shrauger, 1972).
They may also lead to selection of more difficult tasks
(Veroff, 1969) or may keep women from pursuing their desired
career (Jones, Note 5). Thus, the consequences of these
higher male expectations are improved opportunities for their
achievement.

Although males have higher expectations than females,
females generally make more accurate estimations of their
probability of success. When Crandall (1969) compared male
and female expectations for success with predictions based
on objective ability measures, males were found to overestimate their future performances. While the merits of high
expectations have been discussed, the advantages of accurate
estimates are often ignored. If the accuracy of expectations
rather than the absolute level of expectation determined performance, females rather than males might fare better. However, the present culture does not punish over-statement of
ability for males, while it does applaud absolute levels of
performance (Frieze et al., in press-a and b).

Attributing the Causes of One's Own Performance

Research investigating causal attributions for success
and failure has shown that different causal explanations
have varying implications for feelings of pride or shame and
for future expectancies which are similar to the implications
of attributions made by other people. Maximum security in
success is derived from the perception that the success is
due to the internal, stable factor of ability (see Table 1).
Pride, on the other hand, is more associated with success
resulting from trying hard (internal and intentional). However, the effort attribution produces little security about
future successes since continued effort must be exerted to

maintain positive outcomes. Success attributed to external factors produces less pride. If success is perceived as caused by the external, unstable element of luck, there is neither pride nor security that success will reoccur.

An opposite pattern of consequences occurs with failure attributions. Maximum shame is associated with failures perceived as caused by low ability or lack of effort. If lack of ability is seen as the primary cause of the failure, not only is there shame (since this is an internal attribution), but there is also an avoidance of the activity in the future, since the person will believe that there will be no way in which future failure could be avoided (except for occasional instances of good luck). On the other hand, failures attributed to bad luck or task difficulty produce less shame. If bad luck is perceived as the primary cause, future successes would be anticipated as luck fluctuates. Lack of effort, although leading to shame, would be changeable and, therefore, would result in greater expectancy changes than lack of ability attributions.

Although attributions are clearly influenced by situational factors (e.g., Frieze & Weiner, 1971; Snyder & Frieze, Note 6), it is hypothesized that in many cases people have patterns of making certain causal attributions more than others (Frieze, 1976-b; Frieze et al., in press-b). Maximum self-esteem would theoretically be associated with a tendency to make internal, stable attributions for success and external, unstable attributions for failure. Fitch (1970) verifies these hypotheses to some degree with data showing that low self-esteem males attributed success more to internal causes. Although these patterns of perceiving success and failure may perpetuate self-esteem, other data suggests that maximum achievement striving is associated with slightly different patterns of causal attributions. Kukla (1972) demonstrated that high achievement motivated men tend to attribute their successes to both high ability and effort while they perceive their failures as caused by lack of effort. Thus, these men are "motivated" by the experience of failure to try harder. Also, high achievement motivation is generally associated with higher expectancies or estimates of personal ability (Bar-Tal & Frieze, in press; Kukla, 1972). Low achievement motivation is associated with less attribution of success to internal factors; failure for low achievers is more attributed to their low ability (Weiner & Kukla, 1970; Weiner & Potepan, 1970).

Much of this data on individual differences in causal attributions is based only on male subjects (who are college students). However, given the low initial expectancies which women generally report, certain attributional patterns might

be predicted (Frieze et al., in press-b). If a woman expects
to do poorly but instead does well, she would be likely to
attribute the outcome to an unstable cause such as luck.
This means she will not change her expectancies and she feels
no pride in her success if the attribution is made to the
external element of luck. When a female with low expectancy
fails on a task, an expected outcome, she tends to attribute
it to lack of ability. This attributional pattern perpetuates
a Low Expectation Cycle by minimizing the positive effects of
success and maximizing the negative effects of failure
(Jackaway, 1974) which is similar to the Valle and Frieze
(1976) model described earlier for attributions of other
people (see Figure 2).

Some research has supported these predictions that
women would attribute success more to luck and failure more
to lack of ability. This self-derogatory pattern has been
found in grade school girls (Dweck & Reppucci, 1973;
Nicholls, 1975). Also, girls, more than boys, tend to focus
on negative feedback as a basis for deciding how they will do
in the future (Crandall, Katkowsky, & Crandall, 1965). Women
are more likely than men to attribute failures to lack of
ability (McMahan, Note 7). Given such attributions, it is
easy to see why women might avoid achievement situations
since when women make these attributions, the subjective outcome of achievement tasks can at most be neutral (for success)
and may be highly negative (for failure).

However, much of the current research does not find
these attributional patterns in women. Many studies have
instead found a general externality on the part of females
(e.g., McArthur, 1976). Some studies have found that
females rate tasks as easier than do males in both success
and failure conditions (Bar-Tal & Frieze, in press; McMahan,
Note 7). By rating the task as easier after either success
or failure, females may have reduced the value of their
successes, and increased the negative implications of their
failures; thus, these task-ease attributions are similar in
substance to the self-derogatory pattern discussed above
(Frieze et al., in press-b).

A number of studies have found that females make greater
use of luck attributions than males for both success and
failure (Bar-Tal & Frieze, in press; Feather, 1969; McMahan,
Note 7; Simon & Feather, 1973; Weigers & Frieze, in press).
This pattern is also characterized by a general externality,
but has different implications from task-ease attributions.
The pattern of luck attributions implies that, at least within traditionally defined masculine areas assessed in these
studies (such as academic achievement), women take less
responsibility for and feel less pride in their successes and

Table 2

Possible Factors Influencing Expectations
and Attributions of Women

Factor	Typical Direction of Influence
1. Societal Expectations Female Success	Women expected to do poorly on achievement tasks. Success attributed more to luck.
2. Personal Expectations for Success	Women generally have low expectations for themselves. Attribute success more to luck or the task.
3. Individual Differences:	
Achievement Motivation	Highs more internal, believe in effort more.
Fear of Success	Denial of responsibility for success through external attributions.
Androgeny	Higher expectations for masculine tasks. More internal attributions for success.
4. Situational Factors:	
Type of Task—Experience	Higher expectancies for tasks with prior history of success.
Type of Task—Sex Role Relation	Higher expectancies for female than male tasks.
Competition	More external for competitive success.

[From Frieze, Fisher, Hanusa, McHugh, & Valle, in press-b.]

less shame about their failures. Thus, women employing this attributional pattern would experience relatively little affect in achievement situations.

It can be concluded that many different patterns of causal attributions can be found in women. Some of these may be related to other personality measures as shown in Table 2 (Frieze et al., in press-b). One of the most important personality variables for understanding women who choose scientific careers may be achievement motivation. Women with high achievement motivation appear to have a somewhat different pattern of attributions than traditionally oriented women. For example, observations of professional women indicate that they work very hard and are highly motivated to succeed. In fact, some writers (Bird, 1968; Epstein, 1971) suggest that they must actually be better at what they do professionally than their male colleagues in order to experience any career success. Futhermore, professional women perform at this high level without any of the environmental supports which professional men frequently have such as a supportive wife (Frieze, et al., in press-a). This pattern of continuing hard work as a basis for achievement in these women suggests that they may perceive their successes and failures as being dependent upon effort rather than upon luck or other causal factors. However, data indicating that nearly all women have lower estimates of their own abilities than men would also lead to the hypothesis that even high achievement motivated women lack the positive belief in their own abilities which characterizes the high achievement motivated man (Frieze, 1975; Frieze et al., in press-b).

Preliminary studies have suggested that highly motivated women do employ more effort attributions for both success and failure than low achievement motivated women (Feldman-Summers & Kiesler, 1974; Frieze, 1973). Bar-Tal and Frieze (in press) also found that high achievement motivation was related to higher estimates of ability for both male and female subjects although this finding was stronger for men than women. In one of the few studies using a black sample, Murray and Mednick (1975) found that achievement motivation levels affected the causal attributions of black women. Also, there appear to be differential attributional patterns for under and "over achieving" women and men (Weigers & Frieze, in press).

Along with individual differences in attributional patterns among women, there are also a number of situational factors which affect attributions. The fact that attribution patterns may vary for an individual across situations is seldom taken into account. It is generally implied that one's pattern of making causal attributions is an enduring disposition. However, the assumption of such consistency is being generally challenged (Bem & Allen, 1974; Mischel, 1973). A relative lack of interest in situational deter- minants of attribution patterns may be partially responsible for the inconsistencies found in some of the attribution research (Frieze et al., in press-b).

Causal attributions are generally considered an internal process which influences the individual's expectancies and affect in a given situation. Attribution therapy (see Frieze, 1975, or Dweck, 1975) has been suggested as a way of altering female attributions to affect a change in their expectancies and resultant achievement. However, attribu- tions are formed on the basis of the individual's experiences in the external world. If fears of social rejection are realistic and if modesty and/or noncompetitiveness are trained into females, then we cannot expect to change attri- butions without a change in society's values and in the socialization process for children.

Societal Attitudes as a Covert Barrier to Women in Science

Training Women for Nonachievement

Given our traditional expectations for the future roles of girls and boys, it is not surprising that socialization processes push girls toward wife and mother roles while boys are more oriented toward achievement through their future jobs. Children and adults who are most traditional in their sex-role attitudes show the greatest performance differences on sex-typed tasks (e.g., Bem, 1975) and non-traditional girls have higher task expectancies as well as less tradi- tional career aspirations (Wiegers & Frieze, in press).

This differential socialization comes from the home, the schools and the media (Frieze et al., in press-a). However, given the changes which are occurring in women's adult roles, this socialization no longer prepares either sex well for their future roles. Hopefully our training of children will begin to reflect this. The fact that some previously common sex differences are failing to appear in recent studies (Lunneborg & Rosenwood, 1972; Maccoby & Jacklin, 1975) gives us some support that this is happening. Further analyses of cognitive variables such as expectations for success and failure and attributions about the causes of successes and failures will help to document and understand the processes underlying such changes if they are occurring.

Attitudes of Women

One of the groups in which changing attitudes seem to be occurring is in women. College women no longer tend to evaluate the performance levels of women as lower than men. For example, in a replication of the Goldberg study, Morris (Note 8) found that although male subjects rated female authors lower, her female subjects gave higher ratings to female-written articles. This data suggests that some women are becoming more supportive of female achievements and tend to value them more than male achievements, perhaps because of their growing realization of the effort necessary for women to be productive. This supportiveness of women is further seen in a study by Deaux and Taynor (1973). They found that, as in earlier studies, males rated highly competent men higher on intelligence and general competence than comparable women, but that female subjects tended to rate the competent women relatively higher than competent men on competence. Thus, there may be an increasing trend for clearly competent women to be evaluated more favorably by women, but this trend does not seem to be evident in male perceptions of female competency. Therefore women must still achieve within a less supportive environment since most women are evaluated by men rather than by women (Frieze et al., in press-b).

However, the supportiveness of other women is very important since it appears that many women get their greatest support for professional activities from other women. Men frequently cite the importance of older male role models in their own professional development. These men act as models as well as providing tangible help to younger men. Since women are often denied access to these older males, they have often turned to their female peers for this (Douvan, 1976). This may be out of necessity because of the male attitudes toward women (Bernard, 1976) or because the women do not really want to be "one of the boys" by denying the feminine aspects of their lives (Douvan, 1976).

Women's mutual supportiveness may be especially needed in male fields such as science. Men tend to be less supportive than women of women who desire to achieve in fields with few women; this is true for college students (Lockheed, 1975) and faculty (Etaugh, 1973). Also, male students appear to be more similar in their attitudes to their male faculty than women students (Robin, 1969). This again suggests that female students will have less in common with their male faculty mentors.

Role Models

Of course, as more women enter fields such as science, there will be more role models for future women scientists. Several studies suggest that the availability of role models indirectly affects the expectancies of women for themselves. Women whose mothers worked or who had mothers who reinforced the idea of their working tend to have higher estimates of female ability and competence in general (e.g., Broverman et al., 1972). Similarly, mothers who saw themselves as competent and valued achievement in their daughter had daughters with higher feelings of competence (Baruch, 1976). One of the stronger predictive factors for high career aspirations for college women is having a working mother to serve as a role model (Almquist & Angrist, 1971; Astin, 1968; Parsons, Frieze, & Ruble, in press).

Another possibility for change in the vicious circle described earlier by the Valle and Frieze (1976) model is that as more and more women prove themselves to be capable through a gradual process of changing expectancies, there should no longer be the initial low expectancy that so many people still have for women. However, changing others' attitudes is likely to be a very slow process. And there are several basic questions which we still don't know the answer to: Does having a sexist employer make women perform more poorly than they should and is a supportive employer going to encourage better performance? What about teachers and their beliefs about women? How can women break out of the vicious cycle described earlier when employers or others have low expectancies for them? All of these very practical issues should be addressed.

As was discussed several times in this paper, the lower expectancies many people have for women in our culture have led to debilitating patterns of attributions by women about their own performances. The studies reviewed in this paper further suggest that programs which directly affect the causal attributions made by women might be highly beneficial if we want more women in nontraditional fields such as science. An example of such an approach is seen in the work of Dweck (1975). Perhaps the raising of women's expectations and their confidence in their abilities would be a significant step in breaking the low expectancy cycle. This approach, along with the more direct attributional therapy done by Dweck might help to reduce some of the internal barriers to achievement in women. Once this was done, and women were more successful in areas traditionally defined as masculine achievement areas, the expectations and causal attributions of others about women might then also change.

Dual Roles of Women

A final issue for professional women is their responsibility for two roles (see Smith's Chapter in this volume). Most women in our society want to get married and have children. However, working women generally do most of the housework and child care, just as they would if they were not working outside the home (Bryson, Bryson, Licht, & Licht, 1976; Frieze et al., in press-a). Perhaps for this reason, many female scientists do not marry. Simon, Clark and Galway (1969) found that in a sample of 3,000 women who had received their Ph.D.'s between 1958 and 1963, only 50% of the women were married while 95% of a comparable sample of men were married. Other studies have reported similarly high rates of single women in professional jobs (e.g., Birnbaum, 1975; Cuca, 1976; Rossi, 1965).

In addition, those women who do marry have fewer children if they remain active in their profession (Rossi, 1965; Simon et al., 1969). Parenthood affects the professional mother by cutting down on her attendance at scientific meetings, allowing her to work fewer hours, and allowing her to spend less time in her professional social networks (Theodore, 1971). Thus, the image which may well exist for young women today is that if they want a career in science, they will have to sacrifice getting married and/or having children. This may be a difficult choice and undoubtedly remains as another covert barrier to women entering scientific fields.

However, some women do successfully marry and some are even able to have children and remain successful in their careers. We (Frieze, Jacob & Mitroff) are presently conducting a survey of women scientists to find out what personality and situational factors allow them to do this. We suspect that the type of man they marry is especially important. Bailyn (1970) who has been investigating this issue reports that highly career-oriented women are happier if married to more family-oriented men who help with housework but who are still successful in their own careers. Since most women in the sciences who do marry choose professional husbands (Simon et al., 1969), finding a man who has nonprofessional family interests as well as his professional interests may be crucial. In addition to providing help with mechanical housework tasks, he may also tend to be less personally threatened by a successful wife.

Understanding more about the personal lives of women scientists may well be an important step to removing some of the covert barriers we have been discussing.

Reference Notes

1. Frieze, I. H., Knoble, J. M., & Champagne, A. Children's views of science. Unpublished manuscript. Learning Research and Development Center, University of Pittsburgh, 1977.

2. Frieze, I. H., & Knoble, J. M. College students' beliefs about success in science. Manuscript submitted for publication, 1977.

3. McHugh, M. Sex differences in causal attributions: A critical review. Paper presented at the annual meeting of the Eastern Psychological Association, New York, 1975.

4. Lacher, M., & Lacher, M. R. Sex differences in self evaluation of academic achievement and ability. Paper presented at the annual meeting of the Midwestern Psychological Association, 1975.

5. Jones, H. The effects of pre-college counseling on the educational and career aspirations of Blacks and women enrolled at the University of Pittsburgh. Unpublished manuscript, Office of Institutional Research and Planning Studies, University of Pittsburgh, 1973.

6. Snyder, H. N., & Frieze, I. H. The biasing effect of causal belief structures on achievement-related attributions. Manuscript submitted for publication, 1977.

7. McMahan, I. D. Sex differences in causal attribution following success and failure. Paper presented at the annual meeting of the Eastern Psychological Association, 1971.

8. Morris, M. B. Anti-feminism: Some discordant data. Paper presented at the Pacific Sociological Association, April, 1970.

References

Almquist, E. M., & Angrist, S. S. Role model influences on college women's career aspirations. Merrill-Palmer Quarterly, 1971, 17, 263-279.

Alper, T. G. Achievement motivation in college women: A now-you-see-it-now-you-don't phenomenon. American Psychologist, 1974, 29, 194-203.

Astin, H. Factors associated with the participation of the woman doctorate in the labor force. Personal Guidance Journal, 1968, 45, 240-246.

Bar-Tal, D., & Frieze, I. H. Achievement motivation for males and females as a determinant of attributions for success and failure. Sex Roles, in press.

Bailyn, L. Career and family orientation of husbands and wives in relation to marital happiness. Human Relations, 1970, 23, 97-113.

Baruch, G. K. Girls who perceive themselves as competent: Some antecedents and correlates. Psychology of Women Quarterly, 1976, 38-49.

Battle, E. Motivational determinants of academic task persistence. Journal of Personality and Social Psychology, 1965, 2, 205-218.

Bem, D. J., & Allen, A. On predicting some of the people some of the time: The search for cross-situational consistencies in behavior. Psychological Review, 1974, 81, 506-520.

Bem, S. L. Sex role adaptability: One consequence of psychological adrogyny. Journal of Personality and Social Psychology, 1975, 31, 634-661.

Bernard, J. Women and the Public Interest. Chicago: Aldine-Atherton, 1971.

Bernard, J. Where are we now? Some thoughts on the current scene. Psychology of Women Quarterly, 1976, 1, 21-37.

Bird, C. Born Female: The High Cost of Keeping Women Down. New York: David McKay, 1968.

Birnbaum, J. A. Life patterns and self-esteem in gifted family-oriented and career-committed women. In M. T. S. Mednick, S. S. Tangri, & L. W. Hoffman (Eds.), Women and Achievement: Social and Motivational Analyses. Washington, D. C.: Hemisphere Publishers, 1975.

Broverman, I. K., Vogel, S. R., Broverman, D. M., Clarkson, F. E., & Rosenkrantz, P. S. Sex-role stereotypes: A current appraisal. Journal of Social Issues, 1972, 28, 59-78.

Bryson, R. B., Bryson, J. B., Licht, M. H., & Licht, B. G. The professional pair: Husband and wife psychologists. American Psychologist, 1976, 31, 10-16.

Campbell, D. P. The clash between beautiful women and science. In A. Theodore (Ed.), The Professional Woman. Cambridge: Schenkman Publishing Company, 1971.

Centra, J. A. Women, Men and the Doctorate. Princeton: Educational Testing Service, 1974.

Crandall, V. C. Sex differences in expectancy of intellectual and academic reinforcement. In C. P. Smith (Ed.), Achievement-Related Motives in Children. New York: Russell Sage, 1969.

Crandall, V. D., Katkovsky, W., & Crandall, V. J. Children's belief in their own control of reinforcement in intellectual-academic achievement situations. Child Development, 1965, 36, 91-109.

Cuca, A. Women psychologists and marriage: A bad match? APA Monitor, January 1976, 13.

Deaux, K., & Emswiller, T. Explanations of successful performance on sex-linked tasks: What's skill for the male is luck for the female. Journal of Personality and Social Psychology, 1974, 29, 80-85.

Deaux, K., & Taynor, J. Evaluation of male and female ability: Bias works two ways. Psychological Reports, 1973, 32, 261-262.

Diggory, J. Self Evaluation: Concepts and Studies. New York: John Wiley & Sons, 1966.

Douvan, E. The role of models in women's professional development. Psychology of Women Quarterly, 1976, 1, 5-20.

Dweck, C. S. The role of expectations and attributions in the alleviation of learned helplessness. Journal of Personality and Social Psychology, 1975, 31, 674-685.

Dweck, C. S., & Reppucci, N. D. Learned helplessness and reinforcement responsibility in children. Journal of Personality and Social Psychology, 1973, 25, 109-116.

Elig, T., & Frieze, I. H. A multi-dimensional scheme for coding and interpreting perceived causality for success

and failure events: The CSPS. JSAS: Catalog of
Selected Documents in Psychology, 1975, 5, 313.
MS# 1069.

Epstein, C. R. Woman's Place: Options and Limits in Professional Careers. Berkeley: University of California
Press, 1971.

Etaugh, C. F. Attitudes of professionals toward the married
professional woman. Psychological Reports, 1973, 32,
775-780.

Etaugh, C., & Brown, B. Perceiving the causes of success and
failure of male and female performers. Developmental
Psychology, 1975, 11, 103.

Feather, N. T. Attribution of responsibility and valence of
success and failure in relation to initial confidence
and perceived locus of control. Journal of Personality
and Social Psychology, 1969, 13, 129-144.

Feather, N. T., & Simon, J. G. Attribution of responsibility
and valence of outcome in relation to initial confidence
and success and failure of self and other. Journal of
Personality and Social Psychology, 1971-a, 18, 173-188.

Feather, N. T., & Simon, J. G. Causal attributions for
success and failure in relation to expectations of
success based upon selective or manipulative control.
Journal of Personality, 1971-b, 39, 527-541.

Feather, N. T., & Simon, J. G. Reactions to male and female
success and failure in sex-linked occupations:
Impressions of personality, causal attributions, and
perceived likelihood of different consequences. Journal
of Personality and Social Psychology, 1975, 31, 20-31.

Feldman-Summers, S., & Kiesler, S. B. Those who are number
two try harder: The effects of sex on attributions of
causality. Journal of Personality and Social Psychology,
1974, 30, 846-855.

Fitch, G. Effects of self-esteem, perceived performance and
choice on causal attributions. Journal of Personality
and Social Psychology, 1970, 16, 311-315.

Frieze, I. Studies of information processing and the attributional process in achievement-related contexts. Unpublished doctoral dissertation, University of California at Los Angeles, 1973.

Frieze, I. Women's expectations for and causal attributions
    of success and failure. In M. Mednick, S. Tangri, &
    L. Hoffman (Eds.), Women and Achievement: Social and
    Motivational Analyses. Washington, D. C.: Hemisphere
    Publishers, 1975.

Frieze, I. H. Causal attributions and information seeking to
    explain success and failure. Journal of Research in
    Personality, 1976 -a, 10, 293-305.

Frieze, I. H. Information processing and causal attributions
    for success and failure. In J. S. Carroll & J. W. Payne
    (Eds.), Cognition and Social Behavior. Hillsdale, New
    Jersey: Lawrence Erlbaum, 1976 -b.

Frieze, I. H., Parsons, J., Johnson, P. Ruble, D., &
    Zellman, G. Women and Sex Roles: A Social Psychological
    Perspective. New York: W. W. Norton, in press -a.

Frieze, I. H., Fisher, J., Hanusa, B., McHugh, M. C., &
    Valle, V. A. Attributions of the causes of success and
    failure as internal and external barriers to achievement
    in women. In J. Sherman & F. Denmark (Eds.), Psychology
    of Women: Future Directions of Research. New York:
    Psychological Dimensions, in press -b.

Frieze, I. H., & Weiner, B. Cue utilization and attributional
    judgments for success and failure. Journal of
    Personality, 1971, 39, 591-606.

Goldberg, P. Are women prejudiced against women? Trans-
    action, 1968, 5, 28-30.

Heider, F. The Psychology of Interpersonal Relations. New
    York: Wiley, 1958.

Hoffman, L. W. The employment of women, education and
    fertility. The Merrill-Palmer Quarterly, 1974, 20.

Horner, M. S. Toward an understanding of achievement-
    related conflicts in women. Journal of Social Issues,
    1972, 28, 157-175.

Ichheiser, G. Appearances and Realities. San Francisco:
    Jossey-Bass, Inc., 1970.

Jackaway, R. Sex differences in achievement motivation,
    behavior and attributions about success and failure.
    Unpublished doctoral dissertation, SUNY at Albany, 1974.

Kukla, A. Attributional determinants of achievement-related behavior. Journal of Personality and Social Psychology, 1972, 21, 166-174.

Lockheed, M. E. Female motive to avoid success: A psychological barrier or a response to deviancy? Sex Roles, 1975, 1, 41-50.

Lunneborg, P. W., & Rosenwood, L. M. Need affiliation and achievement: Declining sex differences. Psychological Reports, 1972, 31, 795-798.

Maccoby, E. E., & Jacklin, C. N. The Psychology of Sex Differences. Stanford, California: Stanford University Press, 1975.

McArthur, L. Z. Note on sex differences in causal attribution. Psychological Reports, 1976.

McClelland, D. C., Atkinson, J. W., Clark, R. W., & Lowell, E. L. The Achievement Motive. New York: Appleton-Century-Crofts, 1953.

McMahan, I. D. Relationships between causal attributions and expectancy of success. Journal of Personality and Social Psychology, 1973, 28, 108-114.

Mischel, W. Continuity and change in personality. In H. N. Mischel & W. Mischel (Eds.), Readings in Personality. New York: Holt, Rinehart and Winston, 1973.

Murray, S. R., & Mednick, M. T. S. Perceiving the causes of success and failure in achievement: Sex, race and motivational comparisons. Journal of Consulting and Clinical Psychology, 1975, 43, 881-885.

New York Times. Fraud in research is a rising problem in science. January 23, 1977 (p. 1, 44).

Nicholls, J. Causal attributions and other achievement related cognitions: Effects of task, outcome, attainment value and sex. Journal of Personality and Social Psychology, 1975, 31, 379-389.

O'Leary, V. E. Some attitudinal barriers to occupational aspirations in women. Psychological Bulletin, 1974, 81, 809-826.

Parsons, J. E., Frieze, I. H., & Ruble, D. N. Intrapsychic factors influencing career aspirations in college women. Sex Roles, in press.

Pheterson, G. I., Kiesler, S. B., & Goldberg, P. A.
Evaluation of the performance of women as a function of
their sex, achievement and personal history. Journal of
Personality and Social Psychology, 1971, 19, 114–118.

Piacente, B. S., Penner, L. A., Hawkins, H. L., & Cohen,
S. L. Evaluations of the performance of experimenters
as a function of their sex and competence. Journal of
Applied Social Psychology, 1974, 4, 321–329.

Robin, S. S. The female in engineering. In R. Purucci &
J. E. Gerstl, The Engineers and the Social System. New
York: John Wiley, 1969.

Rosenthal, R., & Jacobson, L. R. Teacher expectations of
the disadvantaged. Scientific American, 1968, 218,
19–23.

Rossi, A. S. Women in science: Why so few? Science, 1965,
148, 1196–1202.

Shrauger, J. S. Self-esteem and reactions to being observed
by others. Journal of Personality and Social Psychology,
1972, 24, 92–101.

Simon, J. G., & Feather, N. T. Causal attributions for
success and failure at university examinations. Journal
of Educational Psychology, 1973, 64, 46–56.

Simon, R. J., Clark, S. M., & Galway, K. The women Ph.D.:
A recent profile. Social Problems, 1969, 15, 221–236.

Stein, A. H., & Bailey, M. M. The socialization of achievement orientation in females. Psychological Bulletin,
1973, 80, 345–366.

Tangri, S. S. Determinants of occupational role innovation
among college women. Journal of Social Issues, 1972, 28,
177–200.

Theodore, A. The professional women: Trends and prospects.
In A. Theodore (Ed.), The Professional Woman.
Cambridge: Schenkman Publishing Company, 1971.

Tyler, B. B. Expectancy for eventual success as a factor
in problem solving behavior. Journal of Educational
Psychology, 1958, 49, 166–172.

Valle, V. A. <u>Attributions of stability as a mediator in the changing of expectations</u>. Unpublished doctoral dissertation, University of Pittsburgh, 1974.

Valle, V. A., & Frieze, I. H. The stability of causal attributions as a mediator in changing expectations for success. <u>Journal of Personality and Social Psychology</u>, 1976, <u>33</u>, 579-587.

Veroff, J. Social comparison and the development of achievement motivation. In C. P. Smith (Ed.), <u>Achievement-Related Motives in Children</u>. New York: Russell Sage, 1969.

Weiner, B. Achievement motivation as conceptualized by an attribution theorist. In B. Weiner (Ed.), <u>Achievement Motivation and Attribution Theory</u>. Morristown, New Jersey: General Learning Press, 1974.

Weiner, B., Frieze, I., Kukla, A., Reed, L., Rest, S., & Rosenbaum, R. M. <u>Perceiving the Causes of Success and Failure</u>. New York: General Learning Press Module, 1971.

Weiner, B., Heckhausen, H., Meyer, W., & Cook, R. E. Causal ascriptions and achievement behavior: Conceptual analysis of effort and reanalysis of locus of control. <u>Journal of Personality and Social Psychology</u>, 1972, <u>21</u>, 239-248.

Weiner, B., & Kukla, A. An attributional analysis of achievement motivation. <u>Journal of Personality and Social Psychology</u>, 1970, <u>15</u>, 1-20.

Weiner, B., & Potepan, P. A. Personality correlates and affective reactions toward exams of succeeding and failing college students. <u>Journal of Educational Psychology</u>, 1970, <u>61</u>, 144-151.

Weiner, B., Russell, D., & Lerman, D. Affective consequences of causal attributions. Chapter in J. H. Harvey, W. J. Ickes, & R. F. Kidd (Eds.), <u>New Directions in Attribution Research</u>, Volume 2. Hillsdale, New Jersey: Lawrence Erlbaum, in press.

Wiegers, R. M., & Frieze, I. H. Gender, female traditionality, achievement level and cognitions of success and failure. <u>Psychology of Women Quarterly</u>, in press.

5

Male and Female Leadership Styles: The Double Bind

J. Brad Chapman

In 1901, Sir Henry Maine observed that "the movement of the progressive societies has hitherto been a movement from Status to Contract" (28). As societies moved from the highly structured feudal system, emphasis on the determination of social relationships changed from one of "born status" or "social class" to one of social contract, whereby the desired relationship was an expression of the free wills of the individuals involved. In a business sense, the context of social relationships is "bargained" for through a system of free trade and is legally supported by a comprehensive system of contract law specifying the rights and responsibilities of each party to the relationship. Employment, as a social relationship, should also be determined by a system of free will, where each party negotiates their rights and responsibilities based upon factors other than social status. The intent is amiable; however, similar to the problems encountered in the 1900's with respect to restraint of trade, the practice of determining the initial and continual employment contract is something less than what Maine had envisioned. Granted, individuals are free to negotiate their services devoid of feudal system castes, but are we substituting one set of social status criteria for another? Particularly as it relates to minorities and women, employment relationships continue to be determined, in a large part, by status and not contract. At least, the definition of the contract can be influenced by such superficial status characteristics as sex and color.

In 1964, the federal Civil Rights Act was passed to prohibit discrimination based upon such contextual factors as race, color, religion, national origin, and sex. The underlying assumption of the act is that eliminating discrimination based upon these identified social status factors would increase the contractual opportunities for those persons heretofore discriminated against because of some form of

social prejudice. The intent is laudable, but how realistic
are the assumptions? Because we have fair trade legislation
doesn't guarantee that our society is immune from price
fixing practices, or because our society, at least on the
surface, abhors violence doesn't assure us we will be free
from unjust persecution. The issue of discrimination, like
so many other social issues, is just too complex to expect
its remedy through legal controls. While overt behaviors
can be controlled through legislative edict, an individual's
latent attitudes which give rise to covert discrimination and
prejudicial actions are much more difficult to monitor.

Covert discrimination, as it applies in the context of
this paper, occurs when an individual engages in behaviors
which adversely affect, in a direct or indirect fashion, the
opportunity of women to participate on an equal basis with
their male counterparts in an organization. Covert discrimination includes those surreptitious practices, not readily
apparent or observable, which reflect an individual's prejudices or stereotypes and result in actions implicitly
denying women equal opportunity. Such actions can be found
in an organization's hiring, promotion, training or any
number of other personnel practices and they most generally
occur in situations where a degree of managerial discretion
is required and/or allowed by the law. Since overt discrimination is readily observable and explicitly illegal, most
discrimination which occurs in an organization is by nature
covert. Whether intentional or not, the existence of covert
discrimination which results in adverse career consequences
for women in management is a stigma of our society--a
travesty no progressive society can or should tolerate at
any level.

The intent of the Civil Rights Act of 1964 and subsequent legislation and Executive Orders prohibiting discrimination with respect to all aspects of the employment
relationship is absolutely clear. However, when viewing the
issue of discrimination, one can create the mental image of
an iceberg; one third of its size is clearly visible above
the water, while the other two thirds, considered the most
dangerous part, are neatly concealed below the surface. The
water line represents that often non-discernible distinction
between overt and covert discrimination practices--observable
practices which are unmistakably a violation of the Civil
Rights legislation and latent practices which result in
discrimination but are not readily observable. The courts
can provide a remedy for observable, overt discrimination,
but the issue of covert discrimination remains, by and large,
an issue of judgments. Consider the following illustration.

When Jane Doe seeks employment with the XYZ Corporation, and is turned down in favor of Richard Roe, how does she (the EEOC, or the court) know whether that employer discriminated against Jane because she is a woman? The initial answer is to say: Look at the comparative qualifications of the two applicants. Law review articles can create hypothetical situations in which Jane Doe has 50 positive employment factors, and Richard Roe has but 5 such factors; and the reader is then asked to draw the obvious conclusion of sex discrimination. But in the real world, the comparative qualifications are rarely that clear-cut. Jane may have 25 positive factors and 10 negative ones, while Richard may have 20 positive factors but only 5 negative ones. In that situation, the employer must make a purely subjective choice--one not subject to mathematical calculation. That choice may be based on any number of factors, which may or may not include a bias against women. For the court or the EEOC to step in and decide whether the employer did in fact discriminate is to ask it to do something for which the organization itself may not have the answer (39).

As the above illustration relates, the charge for discrimination involves a subjective determination of the intent to discriminate, even though the EEOC has consistently taken the position that "intent" should not be a deciding factor. The fact remains that discrimination is an intellectual process which is many times the product of an attitude, value or prejudice.

In an attempt to avoid the determination of intent, the scope of EEOC has been defined to include "cases in which the employer is discriminating intentionally, cases in which the employer's past discriminatory practices are carried forward by ostensibly neutral practices in the present, and cases in which an ostensibly neutral employment practice results in a work force containing a smaller percentage of minorities than does the general population" (1, p. 54). As a prescribed remedy for violations in the latter two cases, affirmative action programs were developed and hiring quotas were instituted as a means to improve minority representation in the workforce. Although hiring quotas and affirmative action programs have been attacked on a number of fronts (39), they are generally viewed as viable means of abating the problem of past and current overt discrimination.

However, the theme of this book addresses itself to the broader social issue of covert discrimination--the intentional or unintentional act of subverting the intent of federal Civil Rights legislation. The purpose of this paper is to analyze the factors within an organization and an individual which give rise to and potentially reinforce covert discrimination within a traditional business organization.

Sex-Role Stereotypes: The Basis for Covert Discrimination

Sex-role standards (stereotypes) can be defined as the sum of socially designated behaviors that differentiate between men and women (7). Social sex-role stereotypical expectations result in ascribing a given set of characteristics to men and women which influence our perceptions of expected and accepted behaviors for each group. Although the existence of traditional sex-role stereotypes is being dissipated somewhat by the fluidity of contemporary American society and the elimination of overt dsicrimination based on sex, the existence of sex-role standards continues to be apparent. In a comprehensive review of the literature, and supported by empirical investigation, Broverman, et al., (7) concluded that:

"Our research demonstrates the contemporary existence of clearly defined sex-role stereotypes for men and women contrary to the phenomenon of 'unisex' currently touted in the media. Women are perceived as relatively less competent, less independent, less objective, and less logical than men; men are perceived as lacking interpersonal sensitivity, warmth, and expressiveness in comparison to women. Moreover, stereotypically masculine traits are more often perceived to be desirable than are stereotypically feminine characteristics. Most importantly, both men and women incorporate both the positive and negative traits of the appropriate stereotype into their self-concepts. Since more feminine traits are negatively valued than are masculine traits, women tend to have more negative self-concepts than do men. The tendency for women to denigrate themselves in this manner can be seen as evidence of the powerful social pressures to conform to the sex-role standards of the society.

"The stereotypic differences between men and women described above appear to be accepted by a large segment of our society. Thus college students portray the ideal woman as less competent than the ideal man, and mental health professionals tend to see mature healthy women as more submissive,

less independent, etc., than either mature
healthy men, or adults, sex unspecified. To the
extent that these results reflect societal standards of sex-role behavior, women are clearly put
in a double bind by the fact that different
standards exist for women than for adults. If
women adopt the behaviors specified as desirable
for adults, they risk censure for their failure
to be appropriately feminine; but if they adopt
the behaviors that are designed as feminine, they
are necessarily deficient with respect to the
general standards for adult behavior."   (7)

The existence of sex-role stereotypes has had, and will
continue to have, a detrimental effect on women seeking responsible management positions in many organizations. By and
large, women are not perceived as having the requisite skills
and abilities necessary to perform effectively in management
positions. In a comprehensive study on the relationship
between sex role stereotypes and requisite management characteristics, Virginia Schein (38) found that successful middle
managers are perceived to possess characteristics, attitudes,
and temperaments more commonly ascribed to men in general
than to women in general. For example, the study related
that managers were more similar to men than to women in the
following categories: (1) Emotional Stability, (2) Aggres-
siveness, (3) Leadership Ability, (4) Self-Reliance,
(5) Certainty, (6) Vigor, (7) Desire Responsibility, (8) Seriousness, (9) Objectivity, (10) Knowledge, and (11) Straight-
forwardness, but such behaviors as Understanding, Helpful-
ness, and Intuition were more commonly ascribed to women in
general (39).

In an experimental study of mixed-sex triads, Bond and
Vinacke (6) found that males tended toward exploitive behaviors, while the more successful females, in terms of task
accomplishment, tended toward more accommodative behaviors.
This finding, like so many others, reinforces the sex-role
stereotype depicting women as generally more accommodative
and passive in terms of specific behaviors associated with
task accomplishment in a male environment.

The existence of sex-role stereotypes creates a two-
sided problem--one in that the stereotype itself represents
a source of prejudice with respect to the perceptions of how
a female should behave in an organization, and secondly, the
culturally reinforced stereotypes affect how the female
herself actually behaves and her perception of appropriate
and inappropriate organizational behavior.

For example, Megargee (31) conducted a study on the influence of sex-roles on the manifestation of leadership which deals primarily with sex dominance. His paper investigated how social sex-role prescriptions influence the expression of leadership by High Do (dominance) men and women. Although the findings are not directly related to covert discrimination, the implications represent important considerations for the relationship between sex, leadership style, and sex-role stereotypes.

In his first study, Megargee revealed that when high Do men and women were paired with the same sex, 75 percent of the high Do men and 70 percent of the high Do women took the leadership role. When high Do men were paired with low Do women, 90 percent of the men assumed the leadership role. However, when high Do women were paired with low Do men, only 20 percent of the women assumed a leadership role (31). One could conclude that society does not expect women to express dominance, particularly in situations where women are required to interact with men in order to accomplish specified goals. At least as presented in the above research, women may feel considerable inhibition in forceably expressing themselves and, by default, may adopt a passive role and subsequently reinforce the male assumption that women are incapable of effective leadership within an organization.

Laboratory studies tend to reinforce the existence of stereotypical behavior for both males and females in task-oriented roles. In a study designed to measure an individual's tolerance for dissonance, for example, Steiner and Rogers (41) concluded that: (1) Females made less use of rejection than did males, (2) Females were more inclined to tolerate conflict, and (3) The effect of anxiety upon an individual's choice of dissonance-reducing response depended upon the sex of the individual. Similarly, Vinacke and Gullickson (43) found that in competitive activities, women tended to form coalitions in an accommodative manner while men were more exploitive and used coalitions to gain individual advantages. The tendency on the part of society to ascribe more accommodative behaviors to females will affect how they react in decision-making situations. Accommodative behaviors may be viewed as more compromising and consequently resulting in lower quality decisions--a situation most superiors and subordinates find unacceptable. In other words, the female's stronger need for personal interaction, as perceived by society, will adversely affect how others perceive her decision-making abilities. With respect to the nature of interpersonal interactions in problem solving tasks, Exline (14) concluded that (1) women's messages were significantly more person-oriented than were those of men;

(2) in women's, relative to men's groups, S's whose co-workers were visible requested significantly more personal information than did those whose co-workers were nonvisible; and (3) the need for affiliation was significantly and inversely related to the degree of control over others' behavior attempted in the first message written in the process of group problem-solving. Consequently, one would not expect a woman to initially seek control of another's behavior, particularly if she has a high need for affiliation.

A subsequent study by Exline (15) supported his previous studies and basically concluded, among other things, that females interacted significantly more than their male counterparts. In essence, this study replicated his earlier findings in that need affiliation did not have a significant effect on degree of interaction, although interaction was much greater for high and low need affiliation women than men. Apparently, women feel more comfortable in satisfying their needs for association, friendship, love and affiliation through interpersonal interactions than men in similar situations. This generally fits the stereotype that women tend to be more socially oriented in their relationships, while men are supposed to be more task oriented.

Females are conditioned by societal and cultural pressures to adopt behavioral patterns consonant with society's expectations of how they should behave. Korman (25) indicated that, ceteris paribus, individuals will adopt behavioral roles, and experience satisfaction from these roles, which tend to maximize their sense of cognitive consistency. To the extent that a woman's self-esteem incorporates traditionally feminine stereotypic notions, it is plausible to anticipate that she will be hesitant to engage in behaviors requiring characteristics socially typified as male sex role appropriate (32). If the job environment or organizational culture reinforces the desirability of male characteristics, the female will experience considerable cognitive dissonance which will in turn affect her job performance.

Most cultures attribute dominant, aggressive qualities to males and passive, dependent qualities to females. The existence of these sex-role stereotypes has an insidious effect on the provision of equal employment opportunity prescribed by law. It provides a convenient means for classifying all females, regardless of differentiated abilities, according to a predetermined set of characteristics--characteristics which are generally viewed as undesirable for managerial positions in most organizations.

The fact that sex-role stereotyping is generally
accepted by society and operating male managers is well-
documented (8, 38). The question now becomes, how does
social sex-role stereotyping manifest itself in the form of
covert discrimination? In order to answer this question,
three critical factors of women in business must be considered: Organization Structure and Managerial Attitudes,
Job Design and Selection Processes, and Peer Group Support
and Career Development.

Organization Structure and Managerial Attitudes

The organization structure represents the environment
within which an individual works and, in the broadest sense,
reflects the values and goals of its managers with respect
to the utilization of human resources. The organization can
be viewed as a microcosm of society, reflecting basic societal values, goals, and expectations as perceived by the
organization's management. These values, goals and expectations become part of a managerial philosophy which determines some of the basic characteristics of the organization
and, in essence, the organizational culture. Such factors
as the planning and control processes, organizational hierarchy, technology, job design, and reward structure are
developed to reflect basic management attitudes, and to define organizational hierarchy using the best male role in
mind. It is not difficult to visualize the impact of traditional sex-role stereotypes in management philosophies and
organization structure, and the potential existence of latent
discrimination which is fostered by certain traditional
management assumptions.

For example, the widely held assumptions that women are
by nature submissive, intuitive, accommodative, supportive,
compassionate, and indecisive are inconsistent with the
organization's role profile of the ideal manager or employee.
According to some theorists, the very nature of an organization structure, with its emphasis on authority, planning,
control, coordination, technology, and hierarchy, reflects
a domain more compatible with male rather than female characteristics. The commonly held stereotype that women will
encounter problems in their ability to exercise authority
within an organization, a characteristic which, by virtue of
the continued success of the organization, is undesirable,
will mitigate against the female manager. Supporting this
stereotype, research by Denmark and Diggory indicated, "It
is clear that on the average men are more authoritarian than
women with respect to the leader's exercise of authority and

power in the matter of group goals and control of the behavior of individual members" (13, pp. 867-8).

The model decision-maker, in the operational sense of
creating and functioning within the structure, is described
by Douglas McGregor, a leading management theorist, as
follows:

> "The model of the successful manager in our
> culture is a masculine one. The good manager is
> aggressive, competitive, firm and just. He is
> not feminine, he is not soft and yielding or
> dependent or intuitive in the womanly sense. The
> very expression of emotion is widely viewed as a
> feminine weakness that would interfere with
> effective business processes." (30, p. 23)

How is the profile described by McGregor reflected in basic
managerial attitudes toward women occupying responsible
positions in management? An article in the Harvard Business
Review (7) reported that a majority of the male executives
surveyed had a mildly favorable to mildly unfavorable attitude toward female executives. However, clearly one third
of the respondents felt that women executives had a negative
effect on overall morale and fifty-one percent felt that
women were generally unfit for managerial positions. Perhaps
more revealing, in terms of the traditional male manager's
attitude toward the "proper" role of women in business,
is the fact that eighty-one percent of the practicing male
managers surveyed would not feel comfortable with a female
supervisor. Bass, et al., (4) reinforces this assumption by
indicating that men and women would prefer having male supervisors and would be uncomfortable with a woman supervisor.
Bass further concluded that men regard working women as
having different skills, different habits, and different motivations, which make them undesirable as workers. Men
perceive females in the work environment as having a lack of
dependability. Additionally, men and women have defined
roles governing the nature of their social interaction which
may be awkward in a business sense.

The attitudes expressed above clearly indicate that
managerial positions within an organization are largely considered the male province. Not only do a majority of male
managers indicate they would not appreciate working for a
female supervisor, but they also perceive that others in the
organization would not accept working for a female manager
either. Clearly, the conclusion by Orth and Jacobs (33) that
the major obstacles to equal status for women in the work
place include fixed attitudes, confused career patterns and

outmoded notions of the female's role in our society, is
reflected in other studies. Apparently, these attitudes have
been found to exist throughout organizations. A national
survey conducted by the Bureau of National Affairs indicated
that one of the major problems most firms faced in implement-
ing equal employment opportunity and affirmative action programs was "difficulties in educating supervisors and middle
managers, or in some cases, the entire workforce in the need
for supporting equal employment opportunity efforts" (3).
The problems cited above can permeate any organization,
become part of the organization's culture, and result in
implied personnel policies which covertly discriminate
against women aspiring to managerial positions.

In the course of giving approximately fifteen speeches
in the last two years to predominantly lower level female
managers and professionals, the author of this paper has had
the opportunity to interview a number of very capable women
in management positions in a number of different organizations. Invariably, one of the major problems these practicing women managers encounter is the traditional male
assumption that all women are incapable of leadership and
that most members of an organization would rather not "work
for" a female supervisor. The result of such attitudes as
these is to create an organizational environment where the
female manager is made to feel inferior and inadequate in a
leadership role. Qualified females occupying responsible
leadership positions in an "acting" capacity until a suitable
male replacement is found to fill the position permanently
is not uncommon. In other instances, women subordinates are
asked to train males to assume positions as their superiors.
In this latter case, the inconsistency of the organization to
recognize female competencies on the one hand but not follow
through with commensurate management responsibilities on the
other, helps to reinforce the female dilemma of incompatible
sex-role stereotypes (11).

Many of the women interviewed experienced covert discrimination in different forms. For instance, there are the
classic examples of women being asked to be the recording
secretary for committee meetings while never being asked to
chair the meeting, or the more subtle, but nevertheless
discriminating, suggestions that the female member of the
committee be responsible for performing the secretarial
duties of getting coffee, making copies or typing the report.
Other subliminal attitudes include the belief that women will
do their own clerical chores, refusal of female subordinates
to view the female manager as something other than "one of
the girls," lack of female executive washrooms, and the
belief that women should not "act like" women or display any

emotion or ambition (42). Although on the surface, these
actions or conditions may appear to be harmless enough, the
underlying effect is to shatter the female's self-image and
undermine any attempt she may have of devoiding herself of
the inhibitions fostered by sex-role stereotyping. After
all, only a brave (as viewed by some), or abrasive (as
viewed by many) woman would ever suggest that she chair the
meeting or that someone else, probably a man, be responsible
for coffee!

Even the most enlightened and sympathetic male manager
cannot totally overcome his socially derived attitudes with
respect to the role and function of women in business. In
making personnel decisions, certain attitudinal factors can
unconsciously bias the manager in favor of the male employee.
For example, a manager may not give a second thought to
sending a male employee to an expensive one-week management
training and development workshop in another city, while this
same manager would entertain such issues as family responsibility, company benefits, special travel and living accom-
modations, and length of future employment, etc., before the
decision is made to send an equally deserving female employee
to the same workshop.

Rosen and Jerdee (37) conducted a fairly comprehensive
study of practicing executives to determine the extent to
which unintended bias of female employees can creep into
such critical personnel decisions as selection, retention,
promotion, and career development. Approximately 1,500
executives were asked to evaluate a number of "critical
incidents" and to indicate their recommended personnel decisions for each incident. The incidents involved personnel
decisions ranging from career development to employee retention. There was a male and female version for each of the
eleven incidents used. The eleven incidents were distributed
on the questionnaire so that the participating managers could
not obviously detect the intent of the survey and consequently give the more socially desirable response. The conclu-
sions of the survey are as follows:

1. Managers expect male employees to give top priority
    to their jobs when career demands and family obli-
    gations conflict. They expect female employees to
    sacrifice their careers to family responsibilities.

2. If personal conduct threatens an employee's job,
    managers make greater efforts to retain a valuable
    male employee than the equally qualified female.

3. In selection, promotion, and career-development
   decisions, managers are biased in favor of males.
   (37, p. 47)

When the issues under consideration involve a clear-cut
violation of company policy or rules, as in the issue of
disciplinary action for specific infractions, the question of
sex does not appear to be a significant variable. However,
when the manager's judgment must enter into the decision, for
lack of better criteria, the manager will generally rely on
current personal biases and/or existing sex-role stereotypes.
As Rosen and Jerdee explained, "In the more ambiguous situation illustrated..., where an employee's private life inter-
feres with the job demands, greater deference is shown to the
female employee" (37, p. 53). In other words, managers are
less inclined to "help out" a female employee experiencing
job-family conflict than they are male employees. After all,
isn't the resolution of career-family conflict for the female
manager fairly obvious!

The existence of covert discrimination, either intentional or unintentional, was apparent in management development, promotion, and selection decisions. Also, the
preference for males over females existed primarily in those
situations which were ambiguous enough to require discretion
and independent judgment on the part of the manager. For
example, when a male and female employee both clearly have
the qualifications to be promoted, and the job is explicitly
defined, both will be recommended; however, when an issue
such as job-family relationship enters into the decision and
both the male and female candidates express a strong interest
for maintaining a career-family balance, the male will be
preferred. In other words, in evaluating a statement from a
male or female, such as "I value my family relationships and
would not want the job to conflict with my responsibility as
a husband (wife)," the manager may project his own value
judgments into the situation and make a decision based upon
personal prejudices and widely-held social sex-role stereotypes that tend to favor the male in most work oriented
situations.

From this author's perspective, one of the most critical
areas of covert discrimination involves the issue of female
leadership. Although women currently comprise a significant
portion of the workforce, their absence from leadership positions is quite apparent and highly suspect. About one third
of the current workforce is female, while women occupy only
approximately five percent of the middle level management
positions and less than two percent of the top management
positions (21). The scarcity of women in responsible

leadership positions may be attributed to a number of factors, not the least of which is the issue of social sex-role
stereotypes and covert discrimination.

When asked why females are not more evident in leadership positions, practicing managers generally refer to
stereotypical assumptions that women are either too emotional, passive, or relationship-oriented to be effective
leaders. Certainly these assumptions are supported by lab
studies which indicate females are less inclined than males
to assume a leadership position in the first place (27), and
that leader-behavior descriptions differ for males and
females in leadership positions (36). Based upon a significant amount of research, much of which has been reported
earlier in this paper, one would expect female leaders to
have significantly different leadership styles than their
male colleagues and that female leaders would be less effective in accomplishing group goals. Neither assumption is
completely accurate.

To clarify the question of leadership style for females,
the author conducted a study with Fred Fiedler's widely used
Least-Preferred Co-worker (LPC) instrument to measure leadership styles. The LPC instrument asks the person to describe
his (her) least preferred co-worker from a list of sixteen
bipolar adjectives. The sets of adjectives are opposite
characteristics such as warm-cold, friendly-unfriendly,
pleasant-unpleasant, helpful-frustrating, supportive-hostile,
and so on. An individual who describes his (her) least
preferred co-worker in generally favorable terms (warm,
friendly, helpful, etc.) is considered a high LPC person,
while a low LPC person describes their least preferred co-
worker in generally unfavorable terms.

Fiedler indicates that "a high LPC person derives his
major satisfaction from successful interpersonal relationships, while the low LPC person derives his major satisfaction from task performance" (18). In other words, a high LPC
person may view the task as a means of satisfying his (her)
more prevalent need for fostering good interpersonal relationships, while the low LPC person views the task as an end
in itself. Leadership style, as described by Fiedler,
represents the leader's basic underlying need structure while
the leader's behavior includes those activities and behaviors
associated with getting a job done.

Using practicing male and female managers in a civilian
and military organization as subjects, it was discovered
that: (1) there was no significant difference in male and
female leadership styles in situations where the degree of

task structure, position power, and leader-member relations was comparable, and (2) there were no significant correlations between leadership style and demographic variables such as age, education, tenure or position, for either males or females (10).

Thus, the study found that the basic motivational orientation of the leader, with respect to satisfying basic individual needs through a leadership experience, could not be attributed solely to the leader's sex. However, the implications of sex-role stereotyping are not only important to leadership styles but also to actual leadership behaviors. How a leader behaves, how he or she is expected to behave, and what behavior is appropriate in a given situation may not be the same for men and women.

The influence of sex role stereotyping may be more prevalent with respect to female leadership behaviors. In other words, there may be no significant difference in leadership styles, but how the leader behaves or acts in a leadership position may be influenced by the leader's sex. A basic question is: "Will a female leader exhibit leadership behaviors which are more accommodative, since these behaviors would be an extenion of her perceived societal role, or will she concentrate on task accomplishment, since her continued success in a leadership position is a function of high performance?"

Either approach will give rise to male criticism and serve to reinforce existing sex-role stereotypes. That is, if the female manager adopts accommodative leadership behaviors (behaviors that are often encouraged for male managers) she will be criticized for being "motherly," indecisive, or weak. Conversely, if she adopts task-oriented behaviors, she will be criticized for being pushy, unfeminine and temperamental. Faced with this lose-lose conflict, the woman leader, in all likelihood, will experience extreme frustration and resort to a fairly passive existence in the organization, accepting her role as a mere transient in the mainstream of organizational leadership. The insidious effect of this situation is that considerable management potential is being wasted, not to mention the aspirations and the very lives of females facing this "leadership dilemma." Day and Stogdill concluded that "slow advancement when it occurs on the part of women supervisors is not a result of ineffectiveness or lack of such factors as influence, predictive accuracy, or reconciliation of conflicting demands, but a result of their being females" (12, p. 353).

A number of organizationally related factors contribute to the continued existence of covert discrimination which implicitly deny women the opportunity to become effective leaders and occupy increasingly responsible positions within an organization. Existing managerial attitudes is certainly the most critical of these factors and is essentially the foundation upon which covert discrimination throughout the organization is based. These attitudes are reflected in basic organizational design and manifest themselves in the form of discrimination through a firm's selection process. Sex-typed jobs and the assumptions as to who should occupy these positions is a case in point.

Job Design and Selection Processes

Organization design, in terms of specific job duties and responsibilities, and the individuals filling these positions, reflects the basic sex-role stereotypes prevalent in our society. Staff and clerical positions, for example, are developed to provide support and assistance for the decision-making positions and they are normally afforded considerably less status in terms of prestige and salary than traditional line positions. A cursory examination of any organization reveals the high incidence of women occupying these positions! The existence and acceptance of sex stereotyped jobs within an organization can be attributed to the intended design of the organization and the perceived personal qualifications of the individuals occupying these positions. Certain non-decision-making functions must be performed and, to some, should be performed by women, while the decision-making functions, which require more managerial insight and risk, should be performed by men. Highlighting this situation is the following statement by Margaret Fenn:

"Most decision making involves some risk. Women
have not been taught the skills necessary to state
problems, consider alternatives, and make decisions. They have been taught skills in diagnosing,
but lack the emphasis in skill pattern of decision
making. They do not command respect, and they do
not understand or exercise leadership qualities.
They are not independent enough to exercise choice
and assume the responsibilities that result from
action." (16, p. 24)

The female profile as described by Fenn may well exist in reality, but there is no question that it exists in the mind of many male administrators. For example, after identifying a number of standard variables used by practicing managers to evaluate job applicants, it was found that the perceived

importance of a particular variable was a function of the
applicant's sex (9). The female applicant was perceived as
more of a clerical worker while the male applicant was perceived as more of an administrative management employee.

If certain jobs are perceived to be the explicit domain
of male occupants, and if the selection process involves
some management discretion in evaluating the candidate's qualifications, the potential for covert discrimination is
considerable. Illustrating this point, a study by Fidell of
the hiring practices of 155 academic departments of psychology revealed that men received more tenure track job offers
than women, and the average rank offered, given the same
personal qualifications, was higher for men than for women
(17). Even the Academy isn't immune from such job-sex
stereotyping!

Perhaps a more subtle form of covert discrimination
occurs in the job design and selection processes established
to implement affirmative action programs by placing more
women in "managerial" positions. In the interpretation of
affirmative action policies, many organizations missed the
intent of the law and simply tried to remedy the problem of
too few women managers by increasing the number of females in
jobs classified as managerial. The underlying mentality is
the assumption that if affirmative action reports can show an
increase in the number of women in management positions with
a commensurate increase in salary level, the letter and
spirit of the law is being met. However, goals can be
achieved through different methods. If the number of managerial jobs is held constant and the number of women managers
increases, one can expect that the organization's intentions
are reflecting the spirit of equal employment opportunity.
All too often, however, the organization simply increases the
number of managerial jobs and fills these jobs with women.

Job content now becomes the issue and the vehicle to
continue a policy of covert discrimination, while the job
title represents a subtle expression of anti-woman bias.
Jobs can be created which have, at best, questionable benefit
to the organization or the individual incumbent and which
therefore have very little true managerial responsibility.
Normally, these jobs are staff positions and do not significantly contribute to an individual's career growth and
development. Consequently, the female manager may have a new
"responsible" job as "Assistant Chief Engineer" at a significantly improved salary level, but finds that her career has
not really been enhanced in terms of future promotional opportunity. She has been conveniently "shelved" into a
position that meets affirmative action guidelines and

surreptitiously maintains the status quo within the organization. This objective can also be achieved by upgrading
the job title without significantly altering the job responsibilities. An executive secretary now becomes an "Administrative Assistant" or a clerk becomes a "Data Processing
Analyst." The job responsibilities, or for that matter the
status of the incumbent, have not changed and the female
employee still experiences the same degree of discrimination
and frustration--albeit, at a higher salary level!

The existence of such policies creates two apparent dysfunctional consequences which actually reinforce the potential for covert discrimination. The first is that the female
"managers" become disenchanted and accept the distinction as
second-class citizens in the organization. The futility of
trying to succeed in an organization becomes increasingly
apparent and future attempts to improve one's status will be
aborted. By adopting a low profile in the organization, her
behaviors are consonant with societal and managerial expectations and the attitudes giving rise to social-sex-role
stereotypes are reinforced and actually strengthened. If
the female manager doesn't accept her predestination but
attempts to change organizational policies, she will create
the second major dysfunctional consequence: male resentment.

As mentioned earlier, one of the major problems with
equal employment opportunity programs is educating a majority
of the workforce as to the need for such programs. Obviously, the reference was not made to a majority of the female
workforce! The lack of perceived need for affirmative action
by a significant part of the male workforce reinforces their
prejudice against women managers in general, and those most
recently promoted in particular. The situation becomes critical if the woman happens to have been promoted to a position involving some supervisory relationship, no matter how
indirect, to the disgruntled male employees. The problem is
self-perpetuating and the organizational environment created
is not conducive to satisfying the female manager's needs for
self-assurance, self-confidence and achievement. This situation leads to the second major manifestation of covert
discrimination in many organizations: lack of adequate peer
group support and career development.

Peer Group Support and
Career Development

Although there is some evidence that males believe women
should have the opportunity to pursue careers at any level
and that their esteem is higher for career women than for
"housewives" (24), the existence of traditional sex-role

stereotypes has most significantly manifested itself in the
lack of peer group acceptance and support for the female
manager. Research by Lynch (26) and Hawley (20) has empha-
sized the criticality of peer group support by indicating
that the support of a significant male role model (mentor)
will positively affect a woman's career orientations and
performance. Similarly, Schein (38) alluded to the fact that
absence of a female managerial role model may be a major im-
pediment to successful goal attainment on the part of female
managers. "The successful male manager is more likely to
have a mentor, who takes the younger manager under his wing,
shows him the ropes and exposes him to situations and activities that prepare him for the future" (21, p. 284). The
female manager lacks not only a male mentor but a female role
model as well.

Because of the dearth of female role models in traditional managerial positions, women are forced to seek direction and reinforcement from their male colleagues within the
organization. However, the amount of social reinforcement
provided to promulgate the woman manager's achievement or
success oriented behaviors is lacking. The problem may be in
defining the appropriate area of success or achievement
oriented behavior, appropriateness again being ascribed to
traditional male and female roles in society. Women are not
encouraged, or even expected to succeed in the traditional
male managerial role and any woman who aggressively pursues
her own career interests in this direction will incur the
criticism of male colleagues and society in general. As
Horner indicated:

> "As a whole, society has been unable to reconcile
> personal ambitions, accomplishment and success
> with femininity. The more successful or indepen-
> dent a woman becomes, the more afraid society is
> that she has lost her femininity and therefore,
> must be a failure as a wife and mother." (22,
> p. 55)

One of the results of such an attitude is that not only will
the female manager find little on-the-job reinforcement for
behaviors outside of her traditional role model, but she will
also experience considerable role conflict in an attempt to
reconcile her personal motives for success with the environment within which she works.

Lack of peer group support within an organization is
evident through a number of illustrations, ranging from being
excluded from the informal business discussions occurring
"after hours," to the more malicious attempts to willfully

undermine the credibility and effectiveness of the female
manager. As mentioned earlier, many men simply don't want
to work with women and this attitude appears to be more prevalent among men who have worked or are currently working
with women (4). These attitudes give rise to behaviors which
clearly indicate a male manager's prejudice and lack of
acceptance of female managers. The following statements by
practicing male managers are reflective of such attitudes:

> "Most women don't have organizational ability
> that pertains to their time and their jobs.
> Women are bad leaders."

> "If you want to stop backlash, a girl who is
> promoted better be overly qualified and you'd
> better be sure that's obvious to others."

> "I must admit I look for a woman to promote
> who is like a guy. She's got to perform like
> we do. I want a strong, tough woman, an
> organizer, a decision maker and somebody who
> has proved that she can supervise. I don't
> really look for these until the next generation."

> "I am deeply concerned if I see a woman pro-
> moted when I don't think she is qualified, or
> any person sees it. Then they do one of three
> things. They make a lot of trouble, they be-
> come bitter or they quit."

Any of the above statements, no matter what the context, in-
fers the existence of covert discrimination.

Social norms and reinforced sex-role stereotypes inhibit
the type of formal and informal interaction between male and
female peers which is conducive to building effective working
relationships. The reluctance of male managers to discuss
pertinent organizational issues with female managers, no
matter what the reasons, denies the female access to relevant
information which can significantly affect her job performance and eventually impair her ability to progress within
the organization.

Personnel decisions involving committee assignments,
promotions, transfers, special job assignments and special
training opportunities are based not only upon an individual's qualifications but also upon personal recommendations
from the individual's peers and superiors. It is difficult
to determine the exact weight of personal recommendations on
such decisions but only the most naive would assume they have

no significance. For the woman manager subjected to such covert discrimination, this becomes a critical issue for two reasons. First, the woman **may be initially** denied the opportunity to be considered for promotion simply because she does not have peer group support and hence highly supportive personal recommendations in her behalf. Secondly, by not being recommended for special assignments, training opportunities or transfers, her future career mobility is severely impaired and eventually she will in fact be less qualified for promotion than her male colleagues. As mentioned earlier, in decisions which require some amount of discretion on the part of the manager, the "benefit of the doubt" is usually given to the male. Personal recommendations and peer group support may well be the deciding factor in a number of significant personnel decisions and, because of latent sex discrimination, the female manager may find she doesn't have enough stature in the informal organization to receive favorable recommendations.

The situation described above cannot be overcome unless men recognize and experience the quality contributions women can make to the management process. That is, if men and women with similar competencies, status, and organizational rank are required to formally interact on substantive organizational issues, traditional male prejudices of women will probably decrease. According to Allport (2), a change in attitude, e.g., a man's perception of stereotypical female behavior, will be enhanced if the contact is sanctioned by custom or law.

The organization has a primary responsibility to sanction the prescribed context of male-female interaction and to ensure that the interaction is, in fact, between organizational equals. Interaction between unequals--in this case, unequal in terms of competency or organization rank--merely serves to reinforce existing prejudices and promulgate the female manager dilemma (39). One way to facilitate the interaction of equals is to improve the female's managerial skills through training and development opportunities. However, career development opportunities for women are also replete with the possibility of covert discrimination.

Most men within an organization who have demonstrated ambition and intelligence are identified by management as potential managers and are given the opportunity, through special career development programs, to develop more quickly their managerial and technical skills (21). Women demonstrating the same degree of ambition and intelligence are often denied the opportunity for accelerated career development and consequently find their professional growth in an organization severely limited. Specialized training or education which has heretofore been limited for women can be an effective equalizing factor in the competition for desirable jobs. As one female manager said, "My MBA set me apart in the eyes of my department heads. Professional degrees are the best way for women to break through sexual job discrimination" (44).

One of the major problems associated with the lack of career development opportunities for women is that most women are hired into specific jobs or positions rather than into training positions eventually leading to general management (29). Women are not assumed to be managerial material in the first place and, secondly, their tenure in an organization is assumed to be considerably shorter than for their male counterpart. Consequently, evidence of covert discrimination in career development is suggested when an organization analyzes its male and female managers and finds that the average length of time in subordinate positions is considerably longer for the women than for the men. As Orth and Jacobs so appropriately stated, "A company employing a handful of women at the executive level should recognize a warning flag if it finds that those women moved slowly and arduously through corporate ranks and achieved responsibility through longevity. Such a pattern does not necessarily indicate enlightenment or equal opportunity--it only demonstrates the rewards for endurance" (33, p. 143).

Early in their careers, women are "passed over" for development opportunities. This may occur for a number of reasons, some even justified, but more often it reflects the existence of traditional sex-role stereotypes. In the study by Rosen and Jerdee (37) cited earlier, the researchers found that when a female and a male, both equally qualified, were recommended to participate in a special conference, there was a "significant tendency to pick the young male more often than the young female" (37, p. 54). This finding reinforces the earlier stated sentiments that managers tend to be more supportive of male employees in most critical personnel decisions involving some discretion and independent judgment on the part of management.

Career development and job expertise can also be acquired through on-the-job experience. A manager, through delegation of authority and special job assignments, can significantly contribute to the career development of subordinate managers. However, if the manager is hesitant, for reasons which may or may not involve discrimination, to delegate authority to subordinate female managers, their opportunity for professional growth has been circumvented.

All too often, the remedial, routine, or clerical tasks, which involve no real career growth potential, are delegated to the female managers while the more critical duties are reserved for the subordinate male managers. The end result is obvious; the female cannot demonstrate her competence nor can she experience a breadth of job responsibilities which will contribute to her promotional potential.

Since it is difficult to change existing male attitudes with respect to traditional sex-role stereotypes and since <u>forcing</u> managers to promote and work with female colleagues can actually reinforce prejudice, there is a definite need for training and development programs specifically designed for women, with follow-up programs designed for mixed-sex participation. The author surveyed fifty practicing female managers and found that not only is there considerable support for woman-only training programs but that in past training programs in which they participated with males, they experienced considerable sex-role stereotyping. In response to the question regarding the desirability of management development programs for women only, seventy-five percent of the respondents were in favor of such a program. Generally, the reasons given for supporting segregated training included:

1. Opportunity to relate common problems and to share experience with other women in management.

2. Desire to secure support from other women managers and to understand the changing role of women.

3. Willingness to discuss general management problems more openly without men present and to maintain self-confidence.

4. Opportunity to openly discuss problems that seem to be particular to women managers only.

The theme of the responses definitely relates the desire of a majority of women managers to engage in some development activities without, in their perception, being critically evaluated by their male colleagues, a situation that can exist in mixed-sex training programs.

Training can help minimize the problem of covert discrimination, but it will not eliminate the problem. As long as organizations reinforce the traditional sex-role stereotypes, and as long as managers--men and women alike--are allowed to express their prejudices through covert and often

subversive practices, the issue of discrimination will
continue.

Attitudinal changes relating to the acceptance of women
in business can be painstakingly slow, particularly if the
organization culture tends to reinforce and promulgate an
anti-woman bias. Such biases become part of the very fiber
of an organization and represent a cloak of anonymity for
practicing managers to hide behind. Covert discrimination,
a malignancy in the trust sense of the word, can permeate
an organization and contaminate the firm's recruitment,
training and retention programs. It will be arrested only
when mature men and women can put aside their prejudices,
recognize, accept and have trust in their own competencies,
and actively work for its exposure and elimination.

References

1. Elliot Abrams, "The Quota Commission," Commentary, p. 54, October, 1972.

2. G. W. Allport, The Nature of Prejudice, New York: Doubleday, 1958.

3. ASPA-BNA, "Equal Employment Opportunity and Affirmative Action Programs," Bulletin to Management, Survey Report No. 20, p. 8, December, 1973.

4. Bernard M. Bass, Judith Krusell and Ralph A. Alexander, "Male Managers' Attitudes Toward Working Women," American Behavioral Scientist, 15: 221-236, 1971.

5. Tessa Blackstone and Oliver Fulton, "Sex Discrimination Among University Teachers: A British-American Comparison," The British Journal of Sociology, 26: 261-275, 1975.

6. J. R. Bond and W. E. Vinacke, "Coalitions in Mixed-Sex Triads," Sociometry, 24: 61-75, 1961.

7. G. Bowman, B. N. Wortney, and S. H. Greysen, "Are Women Executives People?" Harvard Business Review, 43: 14-28, 164-178, 1965.

8. Inge K. Broverman, Susan Raymond Vogel, Donald M. Broverman, Frank E. Clarkson, and Paul S. Rosenkrantz, "Sex-Role Stereotypes: A Current Appraisal," Journal of Social Issues, 28: 59-78, 1972.

9. Earl A. Cecil, Robert J. Paul and Robert A. Olins, "Perceived Importance of Selected Variables Used to Evaluate Male and Female Job Applicants," Personnel Psychology, 26: 397-404, 1973.

10. J. Brad Chapman, "Comparison of Male and Female Leadership Styles," Academy of Management Journal, 18: 645-650, 1975.

11. J. Brad Chapman and Fred Luthans, "The Female Leadership Dilemma," Public Personnel Management, 4: 173-179, 1975.

12. D. R. Day and R. M. Stogdill, "Leader Behavior of Male and Female Supervisors: A Comparative Study," Personnel Psychology, 25: 353-360, 1972.

13. Florence L. Denmark and James C. Diggory, "Sex Differences in Attitudes Toward Leader's Display of Authoritarian Behavior," Psychological Reports, Southern University Press, Vol. 18, pp. 867-868, 1966.

14. Ralph V. Exline, "Effects of Need for Affiliation, Sex, and the Sight of Others Upon Initial Communications in Problem-Solving Groups," Journal of Personality, 30: 541-556, 1962.

15. Ralph V. Exline, "Explorations in the Process of Person Perception: Visual Interaction in Relation to Competition, Sex, and Need for Affiliation," Journal of Personality, 31: 1-20, 1963.

16. Margaret Fenn, "Female Dimension: Barriers to Effective Utilization of Women in the World of Work," University of Washington Reprint Series, Winter, p. 24, 1976.

17. L. S. Fidell, "Empirical Verification of Sex Discrimination in Hiring Practices in Psychology," American Psychologist, 25: 1094-1098, 1970.

18. Fred E. Fiedler, A Theory of Leadership Effectiveness, New York: McGraw-Hill, 1967.

19. Mary M. Fuller, "In Business the Generic Pronoun 'He' Is Non-Job Related and Discriminatory," Training and Development Journal, 27: 8-11, 1973.

20. P. Hawley, "What Women Think Men Think," Journal of Counseling Psychology, 3: 193-199, 1971.

21. J. Stephen Heinen, Dorothy McGlauchlin, Constance Legeros and Jean Freeman, "Developing the Woman Manager," Personnel Journal, 282-297, May, 1975.

22. M. S. Horner, "Femininity and Successful Achievement: A Basic Inconsistency," in J. M. Bardwick, E. Donovan, M. S. Horner, and D. Gutmann, Eds., Feminine Personality and Conflict, Belmont, Calif.: Brook-Cole, 1970.

23. A. Robert Kohn and Fred E. Fiedler, "Age and Sex Differences in the Perception of Persons," Sociometry, 24: 157-163, 1961.

24. M. Komarovsky, "Cultural Contradiction and Sex Roles: The Masculine Case," American Journal of Sociology, 78: 873-884, 1973.

25. H. K. Korman, "Toward a Hypothesis of Work Behavior," Journal of Applied Psychology, 54: 31-41, 1970.

26. E. M. Lynch, The Executive Suite: Feminine Style, New York: AMACOM, 1973.

27. N. R. F. Maier, "Male Versus Female Discussion Leaders," Personnel Psychology, 23: 455-461, 1970.

28. Maine, Ancient Law, London, pp. 168-170, 1901.

29. Bird McCord, "Identifying and Developing Women for Management Positions," Training and Development Journal, 25: 2-5, 1971.

30. D. McGregor, The Professional Manager, New York: McGraw-Hill, 1967.

31. Edwin I. Megargee, "Influence of Sex Roles on the Manifestation of Leadership," Journal of Applied Psychology, 53: 377-382, 1969.

32. Virginia E. O'Leary, "Some Attitudinal Barriers to Occupational Aspirations in Women," Psychological Bulletin, 81: 809-826, 1974.

33. Charles D. Orth, 3rd and Frederic Jacobs, "Women in Management: Pattern for Change," Harvard Business Review, p. 139-147, July/August, 1971.

34. Richard N. Osborn and William M. Vicars, "Sex Stereotypes: An Artifact in Leader Behavior and Subordinate Satisfaction Analysis?" Academy of Management Journal, 19: 439-449, 1976.

35. Gail I. Pheterson, Sara B. Kiesler and Philip A. Goldberg, "Evaluation of the Performance of Women as a Function of Their Sex, Achievement, and Personal History," Journal of Personality and Social Psychology, 19: 114-118, 1971.

36. Benson Rosen and Thomas H. Jerdee, "The Influence of Sex-Role Stereotypes on Evaluations of Male and Female Supervisory Behavior," Journal of Applied Psychology, 57: 44-48, 1973.

37. Benson Rosen and Thomas H. Jerdee, "Sex Stereotyping in the Executive Suite," Harvard Business Review, 52: 45-58, 1974.

38. Virginia Ellen Schein, "The Relationship Between Sex
     Role Stereotypes and Requisite Management Character-
     istics," Journal of Applied Psychology, 57: 95-100,
     April, 1973.

39. Butler D. Shaffer and J. Brad Chapman, "Hiring Quotas--
     Will They Work?" Labor Law Journal, 26: 152-162, 1975.

40. Bette Ann Stead, "The Semantics of Sex Discrimination,"
     Business Horizons, 5: 21-25, 1975.

41. Ivan D. Steiner and Evan D. Rogers, "Alternative Res-
     ponses to Dissonance," Journal of Abnormal and Social
     Psychology, 66: 128-136, 1963.

42. Richard Allen Stull, "New Answers to an Old Question:
     Woman's Place is in the What?" Personnel Journal,
     52: 31-35, 1973.

43. W. Edgar Vinacke and Gary R. Gullickson, "Age and Sex
     Differences in the Formation of Coalitions," Child
     Development, 35: 1217-31, 1964.

44. _____, Forbes, "My Son the MBA," p. 41-44, March 1,
     1977.